Teaching Music
in the Secondary School

David Bray

Heinemann Educational Publishers
Halley Court, Jordan Hill, Oxford, OX2 8EJ
a division of Reed Educational & Professional Publishing Ltd

OXFORD MELBOURNE AUCKLAND
JOHANNESBURG BLANTYRE GABORONE
IBADAN PORTSMOUTH NH(USA) CHICAGO

Text © David Bray, 2000
First published in 2000

04 03 02
9 8 7 6 5 4 3

British Library Cataloguing in Publication Data
A catalogue record for this book is available from the British Library

ISBN 0 435 809229

Typeset by Saxon Graphics Ltd, Derby
Printed and bound in Great Britain by Biddles Ltd, Guildford

Acknowledgements
The publishers have made every effort to trace the copyright holders, but if they have
inadvertently overlooked any, they will be pleased to make the necessary arrangements at the
first opportunity

Tel: 01865 888058 www.heinemann.co.uk

Preface

Wherein lies the power of songs? ... Song shows us a world that is worthy of our yearning, it shows us our selves as they might be, if we were worthy of the world.

Salman Rushdie – *The Ground Beneath Her Feet*

This book is written as a practical guide for classroom teachers. It is intended to set a context for music education in secondary schools today and also to look forward to future developments. Each chapter sets out an aim and concludes with a summary of the most important points made. The book can be read from start to finish or individual chapters can be accessed as required. There is considerable overlap between the ideas in each chapter and on several occasions the reader will be referred to important points made elsewhere.

I would like to express particular thanks to the following people for helpful suggestions over content or wording: Sharon Green, Janet Mills, Keith Smalley, John Paynter and Julian Nietrezbka. I am also grateful to the many inspirational teachers whom I have been fortunate enough to observe, work with or talk to. Additionally my thanks go to the many students I have taught and the ones I continue to teach. I hope that I am still learning.

This book is dedicated to Benjamin.

Contents

The effective music department in the 21st century

Aim: this chapter sets a context for music education in schools today and offers suggestions for some of the attributes which may be displayed by a 'successful' department in the future.

A context for music in secondary schools

Moving into a new millennium feels significant and provides an opportunity to review where we are and where we hope to be. Any consideration of the future needs to make due reference to the past as well in order to provide contextual information. Although there is not the space here to consider a full history of secondary music education in this country, there have undoubtedly been some key developments and texts which have shaped the direction of music in schools. For example:

- *A Basis for Music Education* (Swanwick 1979)
- *Music 5–16* (HMI 1985)
- various versions of the National Curriculum Orders for music (now published by the Qualifications and Curriculum Authority)
- The Office for Standards in Education (OFSTED) has published regular information on music education in secondary schools, informed by their programme of inspections.

These and other publications provide an insight into important moments in the history of music education in this country. We are often considered to be at the forefront of music education. Colleagues from abroad regularly look at our work with envy and admiration. That they do so is the result of many talented and creative people, working in different fields. The contribution of the academic community has been very strong, the work of Local Education Authorities and government organizations (such as Her Majesty's Inspectors) has also been of crucial importance. Finally, and most importantly, we have benefited from many gifted and visionary teachers.

Music in the secondary school curriculum

One of the most influential books of the 1980s was *Music in the Secondary School Curriculum* (Paynter 1982). This has two specific merits for the purposes of this publication. It was very influential and it was dedicated to precisely the subject under consideration here – the secondary school music department. It is therefore an ideal reference point for the purposes of this chapter, providing an insight into secondary music education in the relatively recent past. Like all the authors mentioned, Paynter has continued to develop and adapt his ideas and to make outstanding contributions to the development of music education in this country. His ideas have developed further since 1982 and his current work is still of immense importance.

Music in the Secondary School Curriculum was a summation of the work of the Schools Council Project of the same name. The book started with six 'guiding principles'. They are summarized here:

- music has a place as a curriculum activity for all students within a broader arts entitlement (in order to develop imagination, sensitivity, inventiveness and delight)
- classroom music is the core activity and extra-curricular music should develop from here
- music takes many forms and can be accessed through many styles
- musical experience is primarily a way of working with sounds and most students have an interest in some type of music
- music is a creative art and requires the exercise of imagination
- music making is more important than musical information.

These 'principles' seem perfectly relevant today. We might want to add:

- ensuring that all students make good progress and reach appropriate levels of attainment (reflecting the changing political climate and increasing emphasis that has been placed on this during the last ten years).

These 'principles' provide an interesting insight into the health of music education at the time. What were the key issues facing music teachers then and how far are they still relevant today?

Examination syllabuses

In 1982 examination syllabuses were undergoing change. There were plans to move from GCE and CSE exams to a single 16+ exam. The General Certificate in Secondary Education (GCSE) examination is now well established and teachers' inevitable early concerns about change have largely been resolved. There are many who consider the introduction of GCSE to have been a success and significantly more students now take GCSE music than GCE O level and CSE combined (see chapter eight). The GCSE course represents a broader, often more practical approach to music than was found in the more traditional O level syllabus, and makes music accessible to a wider range of students. However, despite this success, there is still room for further development:

■ there is some difference of opinion, even now, about how obtainable a 'C' grade pass is (currently considered a significant measure of achievement) for those students who have not received extra tuition outside class music lessons. There are some teachers who would regard an A* or A grade as a perfectly feasible target for a student, regardless of whether or not they had received any extra tuition outside class lessons. This is a particularly important point since if a 'good' pass is not accessible to those students who have not received extra tuition outside class lessons this will make music a unique subject within the secondary curriculum. This fact may also contribute to debate about how students who receive extra tuition are selected (since a selection procedure at the age of nine could, potentially, have an impact on a student's chances of success at examination aged 16, or option choices at 14). For more information on selection see chapter seven.
■ should we be aiming to increase the number of students who wish to take GCSE above the current average of 7% of the school population (which, compared to other optional subjects, is a relatively low number)? For more information see chapter eight. We know that other comparable subjects (for example *drama and art*) attract significantly more students. We also know that very few students go on to take music as an examination subject post-16.

We can note a corollary with recent developments of A level specifications. It is generally accepted that we should be encouraging post-16 curriculum students to take a broader range of subjects. One outcome of this process is that more students may take AS music, or other accredited courses. A broadening of curriculum content could also help to attract a wider range, and therefore number, of students. This process mirrors closely that which informed the changes to GCSE courses in the 1980s.

Class music and out-of-class music

There has been a consistent difficulty between the role of music as a curriculum subject and the strong identity it exhibits out-of-class. Tensions often arise because of the relatively small numbers involved in out-of-class activities, the amount of esteem given to them by senior managers and the sometimes disproportionate amount of time and effort they demand from the teacher. Paynter (1982: 15) pointed this out:

> *The more we exploit the opportunities for extra-curricular ensembles and encourage the talented students to increase their skills, the less spin-off there may be within the curriculum as a whole. As we have seen, other pressures may force teachers to give extra attention to the musically talented and so slant the programme towards the 'out of class' activities anyway. Where this happens it is not uncommon to find that, far from causing others to want to join in, musical activities assume an exclusive appearance, with a correspondingly weakening effect upon general class music.*

There is probably a greater expectation today than ever before that the music curriculum will be effectively planned and taught. Music teachers, along with their other colleagues, are expected to produce schemes of work, contribute to whole-school developments, have effective assessment policies and do all the things required of any middle manager. There has not been, however, a decline in expectations for the music teacher's commitment to out-of-class activities. A brief glance at job advertisements in the *Times Educational Supplement* provides an insight into the importance given to these extra activities when making appointments. This can put enormous pressure on the teacher and lead to some conflicts of loyalty.

There are probably two factors at work here. The first relates to the training and background of most music teachers, including instrumental teachers working privately and within Local Education Authorities. Most specialist music teachers probably become interested in music through learning an instrument. This interest might involve participation in extra-curricular music groups, specialist study at A level and then higher education. A strong component in these experiences is likely to be performance on a chosen instrument and participation in a range of ensembles. This instrumental music education will most probably have centred on Western, classical music styles. When these students become teachers, whether class teachers or instrumental specialists, it is not surprising that the students who appear easiest to relate to, and worthy of extra attention, are those who are following a similar kind of initiation as themselves.

This situation is further compounded by public reaction to these activities. In *Living School Music*, William Salaman (1983: 1) describes this as the 'Kapellmeister' effect.

> *As Kapellmeister, I organized the talented and interested students into choirs and orchestras and gathered audiences from time to time to witness the results. The headmaster, the parents and my colleagues appeared to value my Kapellmeister's duties more highly than the other. Rarely was I asked by anyone about the classwork, yet a concert or carol service would generate kind comments and congratulations.*

Once immersed in the world of extra curricular music making, it can be difficult for music teachers to make sense of their role within school. They realize, perhaps with a sense of guilt, that they ought to meet the needs of all young people. However they get praise, kudos and sometimes promotion from working with a small number of selected students. What is more this is a responsive and motivated group.

The role of music in schools

A second, more subtle and deeply embedded factor may be at work. It concerns the function of music within schools and reflects a culture that has developed over a considerable period of time. Although its roots are deep they can be difficult to identify. For example *in schools we can find music taking an important role in:*

- assemblies
- 'important' occasions (such as presentation evenings)
- other settings such as fêtes.

In these examples music adds an important element to the experience. It may make a powerful contribution to spiritual, cultural and social development. But how far do these activities contribute to music education?

    In an assembly music is used as a medium for social cohesion, through hymn singing or listening on arrival and departure. Some of the music may be live (for example *the school orchestra or some soloists*). The music will often add atmosphere and in denominational schools the music can make a very strong contribution to worship. Unless planned very carefully these activities are not likely to contribute to musical development, or increased attainment. A school wishing to include this kind of activity as an example of music education would need to consider carefully exactly how this had been achieved. For example *it is only through an element of rehearsal, reflection or appraising activity for all students that this is likely to be possible.* There would need to be some identifiable outcome. It is much more likely that, although music had enhanced the occasion, there was little identifiable education through music taking place. This does not matter, provided that a school does not consider this kind of activity to be a particularly important part of the musical education of its young people and therefore lead it to neglect other aspects of the music curriculum. This sometimes happens.

    'Important' occasions such as presentation evenings usually involve a very small minority of students. Once again the music has the potential to add a powerful ingredient to the occasion. The motive behind the activity is often one of presenting an image to an external audience. It is the kind of image which is often to be found in glossy publicity materials for schools. A certain type of musical activity is seen as a desirable selling point for a school. It has high status and suggests quality, tradition, value and a particular cultural stance. The stance is Western and usually middle class. This activity may only make a limited contribution to the musical development of the relatively few young people involved. Any beneficial effect on the audience would be very difficult to monitor. Effective musical development of the performers would need rehearsals to be organized in such a way that students make quality musical decisions themselves, or so that they were encouraged to think about their performances in a musical way. This kind of approach is still quite rare.

Other events, such as fêtes, are similar to those of the 'important' occasion. However, the role of the music is often not ceremonial but more one of providing an entertaining backwash of sound. Outdoor performances often struggle to maintain subtlety of phrasing or dynamics. These kind of occasions probably have very little to do with musical education for performers or listeners. However, head teachers and governors may expect these activities and value them highly.

Some activities may have an effect on listeners that were not planned or intended. For example *the solo pianist performing a grade 5 piece in the school concert, despite the fact that this musical experience has been gained outside school.* We should be mindful that this might encourage the audience assumption that it is somehow related to the school music department. Does this help to discourage staff, parents and the wider community from becoming sufficiently aware of, or value, curriculum activities?

The purpose of music in schools

Although music has an important role to play during these, and other occasions, it might be helpful to think of these activities as falling outside the core purpose of musical education in schools. The core purpose in this sense would be the general musical education of all students through class lessons. If these extra activities are felt to be important they will consequently require extra time, staffing and resources so that core activities do not suffer. Alternatively they might be treated as a separate, but related, school activity taking place in out-of-school hours (and for which the teachers involved receive extra payment).

Following this line of argument we can see a sort of continuum of activity, with what many would regard as the key purpose of music education drifting away the further along the continuum you travel:

class music lessons (involves all students regardless of prior experience)	school concert of pieces composed for GCSE coursework (part of the school curriculum and all students have the opportunity to opt for this course)	choir performing at open evening (all students have the opportunity to join the choir	school band playing in a school concert (students have to play a musical instrument, for which there is a selection procedure)	school band playing at a school fete (limited musical impact for performer and listener)

This is an important but difficult area to resolve. There are three main strategies that can be adopted:

1. Try to satisfy the whole spectrum as far as possible.
2. Concentrate on the core curriculum and let some students find extra opportunities out of school.
3. Concentrate on the students who have been selected to play instruments and provide opportunities for them to achieve high levels of attainment.

Examples of all these approaches can be found in schools around the country.

Most of us would acknowledge these tensions and difficulties. They are not new and teachers are very much left to make their own decisions about them as best they can.

Music within Local Education Authorities

These difficulties can affect larger structures, such as a Local Education Authority (LEA), as well:

> There are, for example, areas of the country where the Youth Orchestra figures so large in the Authority's view of 'school music' that individual teachers can be forgiven for thinking that their prime duty seems to be to ensure the continuing supply of suitable recruits for the orchestra.

(Paynter 1982: 16)

Things have probably improved. We undoubtedly want students to have the opportunity to aspire to the very highest standards. Support for these activities is very strong. The Youth Orchestra, in particular, seems to attract public favour. It is clearly regarded as a high status activity and its supporters often know how to lobby for support. The supporters are often made up of white, middle-class parents and politicians. Centrally organized activities give powerful messages about music making, since they provide role models and a cultural context for many schools. There is still often relatively little thought given to the sort of influence that centrally organized activity can have on a local community. For example *if a local music service gives a high priority to Western classical instrumental ensembles, instrumental teaching and very little attention to curriculum support it would be surprising if schools were not influenced in some way. The approach of the music service may have come about through historical models, the views of individual teachers or other factors. Many of these may stretch back over several years.*

Many innovative and influential curriculum developments have resulted from the work of effective LEA inspectors and advisers. This was especially the case prior to local financial management of schools. Today there is still much good curriculum support from LEA services and private companies or individuals. There is probably a lack of consistency in this type of support across the country. LEAs have been under financial pressure and have needed to make priorities about which services they will support. Their priorities have most often been the 'high status' central ensembles and groups. Pressures on LEAs to rationalize and prioritize may result in a culture which:

- assumes centrally organized music activity and support needs to be organized exclusively around perpetuating a particular ensemble
- mitigates against a broader and more inclusive ways of thinking.

It is possible and desirable to have inclusion and high standards as dual, complementary aspirations. This is exactly what we would wish to find in schools and there is no reason why LEAs should not aspire to this as well.

At the time of writing, instrumental music teaching has witnessed change. Most of this has revolved around funding arrangements, often as a result of schools having increasing control over their own budgets. The things most lacking in the funding of instrumental tuition appear to be consistency of provision, co-ordination and strategic direction.

Curriculum development

Many teachers interpreted the work of the 1982 'Schools Council Music Project' with enthusiasm. The result was often a more egalitarian philosophy about music education and classroom activities. There seemed to be a feeling that music could be for anyone, not just those who were thought of as being 'musical'. Greater emphasis was given to timbre and texture, perhaps reflecting the style of contemporary music. This enabled more students to feel involved (rather than excluded) and led to some imaginative curriculum development. It also led, in some instances, to a lack of challenge and ambition for the skills expected from secondary students. For example *it resulted in some Year 9 students undertaking activities that required few skills and which were really more appropriate for Year 3 students*. Our expectations have changed and moved on since 1982.

The changing curriculum

How has the curriculum changed? At present music is a National Curriculum 'foundation' subject and a curriculum entitlement for all students up to the end of Year 9. Some would view this as detrimental, since it has meant a degree of centrally imposed conformity and curriculum content. The teacher has lost a degree of autonomy in most aspects of school life. Although music is probably seen as having a lower status than the more important 'core' subjects of English, mathematics and science, its inclusion within the National Curriculum has meant that its place in the curriculum is now more secure than ever before. Reasons for this are complex and there is insufficient space for a comprehensive exploration here. It is perhaps fair to comment that in 1982, before the introduction of the National Curriculum, music teachers were more likely to be asked to justify why music should be included as a curriculum subject. Today we are more likely to start from an assumption that music will be on the timetable. Clearly there is an argument for viewing this as progress. Yet we are constantly mindful of our vulnerability. Music still appears not to be seen by students or parents as a popular subject. Mathematics or science might not be popular, or enjoyable, but they are seen as having vocational relevance and consequent credibility. Music educators rightly convince themselves of the importance of music, the skills it develops in young people and the vocational relevance of the multi-million pound music industry. Our 'customers' do not seem to agree and there is a job still to be done in improving our ability to connect with the majority rather than the minority.

Another factor in our changing expectations has occurred as a result of the introduction of a programme of school inspections, organized by the Office for Standards in Education (OFSTED). The inspection programme is part of a central government drive to make schools more accountable. An outcome has been that OFSTED-trained inspectors inspect all schools as part of a regular programme. Although the model is not radically different from that operated previously by HMI the quantity and frequency of inspections has increased greatly. The reaction from teachers and the public is also more intense. Opinions are likely to be divided over the desirability of the inspection programme. There are those who will regard the whole process as anathema and some, probably a minority, who welcome it. One outcome of the process may be the clear emphasis given to the curriculum (whilst acknowledging the contribution of out-of-class activities) in the majority of reports. There has also been an expectation that music will be inspected using an identical framework to other subjects. Music is not therefore a special case and questions are asked about the attainment of students in relation to what might be expected for their age, the progress they have made and how these outcomes have been affected by the quality of the teaching received. This is a more rigorous approach to certain aspects of the subject than many teachers have previously experienced. In conjunction with a National Curriculum this seems to have put pressure on music teachers to consider their curriculum responsibilities and sharpened debate about some of the purposes of music education. Some have welcomed this; others have viewed it as central control and interference.

New technology

A very significant change since 1982 is the introduction of new technology into the classroom. Computers and related software have affected all aspects of our lives. Although having great potential benefits for music education, technology seems, as yet, to have made relatively little impact in the majority of music classrooms. The principal reasons appear to be:

- lack of access to sufficient quantities of equipment
- teachers' lack of confidence
- the unsuitability of much software produced for the leisure market and the fact that very little is produced specifically for education.

An example of the impact that new technology can have in classrooms is provided by the electronic keyboard. Large numbers have been introduced into the curriculum and this 'simple' technology has had a major impact on music teaching. Some would argue that this change has not been beneficial. It is likely, that as other technologies become cheaper and more readily available, they will have equally telling effects. We can see this happening already in other curriculum areas and in the ways that schools are adapting their curriculum, accommodation and learning resources in response to the opportunities provided by new technology. The potential for Information and Communications Technology (ICT) seems enormous. The government is particularly keen to take this agenda forward and has introduced a number of initiatives such as the National Grid for Learning and the New Opportunities Funded training in ICT for all teachers. For further information on the use of ICT in music education see chapter six.

Music, culture and society

Most young people like music. They enjoy listening to music and will spend relatively large sums of money buying recordings or attending concerts. The media is full of music used to enhance television, film and sell products as part of advertising promotions. Music is everywhere; it is readily available and seemingly particularly valued by students of secondary school age. The same cannot be said to be the case for music in schools. Although primary age students apparently enjoy it by the end of Year 9 it is not popular – when measured by the numbers opting for it as an examination subject and when students are surveyed on their attitudes to subjects. There appears to be a gulf between the music young people enjoy and the music they encounter in school. There are exceptions:

- groups of students who are heavily immersed in school bands, orchestras and choirs appear to identify very strongly with music and to engage with music in schools. They are usually a minority of the school population
- schools which manage to embrace a wide range of styles and cultures, both within the curriculum and in out-of-class activities.

Other, seemingly similar subjects appear to have resolved some of these problems. Drama and art both seem to be more attractive to adolescents. Certainly in terms of option choices at fourteen they attract considerably more numbers than music. We can only speculate why this might be:

- the curriculum offered to students in art and drama during Key Stage 3 is more appealing and more attuned to students' interests. This means that students enjoy these subjects more and therefore want to take them as options after the age of fourteen
- music in schools tends to concentrate on Western classical styles which are viewed as alien or unappealing by the majority of Key Stage 3 students. Art and drama may have avoided this trap by ensuring that they embrace far more than great works of the theatre (for example *Shakespeare*) or the work of the 'masters' (*such as Rembrandt or Leonardo da Vinci*)
- music teachers may actively discourage students who have not received extra tuition on instruments. They may not do this consciously but inadvertently give the impression that to be a musician a student will need talent, experience of learning an instrument or graded music examinations
- art and drama may be seen as having greater vocational relevance for students. This may not be true but students and their parents, who are often influential in suggesting option choices and career aspirations, may have gained this impression.

It is possible that students do not want 'their' music to have any part in the life of schools. This would represent a contamination of a culture that draws its strength from its alternative nature. Once absorbed into the mainstream it may risk losing its excitement and decadence. Popular music may be seen by many who have influence in schools as a lower form of cultural experience. Governors and senior managers may not value this kind of music as highly as the Western classical tradition, particularly when they wish to promote an image of a school as a guardian of quality and standards.

New technology may force music teachers to confront these problems. Computers, sound modules and related software will probably mean that the sound world of popular music is readily available in secondary classrooms. Once students gain access to resources that replicate the music they can hear on radio or CD and are able to download resources easily from the Internet there may be no going back. The culture of music in secondary classrooms may be changing as a result of technology. An outcome may be that music can become a more popular curriculum subject. This will require a radically new approach by many of us and has big implications for initial teacher training and continual professional development needs.

◤ The future

Having spent some time setting out a brief context for music education in school today it is time to consider the music department of the future. This might provide a useful starting point for an audit of where your school is at present. See chapter eleven for more information on self-review.

What are the features we would want to see in an effective music department in the 21st century?

1. All students, regardless of prior experience or capability, are engaged in active music making and are allowed to feel a sense of achievement.
2. In most schools Key Stage 3 students achieve levels which are in line with, or above expectation for their age. For example *the attainment of students in music matches, or exceeds, the profile of students' attainment in other subjects in the school.* In some schools attainment will be either above or below that generally expected. This will reflect the prior experiences of these students. In relation to this experience students make good progress.
3. The attainment of boys and girls is broadly similar.
4. The attainment of different ethnic groups is not significantly different from the general school population.

5. Uptake rates for GCSE courses are high i.e. *above 10% of the school cohort but may well be nearer 20%, or matching other optional subjects such as art and drama.* Students achieve GCSE examination results that match or exceed their attainment in other subjects.
6. Uptake rates for A level and other post-16 courses match other subjects in the school. Students achieve results that match or exceed their attainment in other subjects.
7. The music curriculum responds to the cultural heritage of the local community, whilst addressing a range of other cultures.
8. The curriculum promotes the musical achievements of different cultural groups and both sexes.
9. Good information is provided on musical opportunities within the local and wider community.
10. Good information is provided on study opportunities post-16 and in higher education.
11. Good information is provided on career opportunities where music qualifications are relevant.
12. Students have the opportunity to learn a range of musical instruments, which reflect their interests and aspirations.
13. Opportunities are provided for students to perform in out-of-class music activities.
14. Out-of-class and in-class music making is integrated and complementary.
15. The music department is well resourced and ICT is used to enable students to make progress (and not used when other resources are more appropriate).
16. Music makes an important contribution to the life of the school and to the development of key skills (for example *social, moral and spiritual development, literacy, ICT* and so on).

Summary points:
- Music education has continued to develop greatly and is held in high regard internationally. This is the result of a strong academic community, influential writers, government departments and effective teachers.
- There is still a tension between music as a curriculum subject for all students and music as an out-of-class activity for a smaller number.
- Continuing demands are being made on teachers and the music department of the future will need to exhibit some key features. These are challenging but in-line with expectations for other subjects.

2

Planning schemes of work

Aim: this chapter provides a model for planning a scheme of work. There are other models, which are equally effective. An effective scheme of work will need to fulfil some key criteria. These are discussed.

◆ Introduction

The phrase 'scheme of work' tends to be interpreted in different ways. At one end of the spectrum is a document that includes detailed lessons plans for every topic to be covered. The other end is much more minimalist and gives a broader picture. There is, of course, a level in-between. These levels of planning are often described as short, medium or long-term:

- **Long-term planning:** gives key information about what students should know, understand and be able to do by the end of a year, Key Stage or examination course. It probably does not include any detail about individual lessons and is expressed mostly in terms of the intended learning outcomes (i.e. what the students will have achieved at the end of a period of time). This level of planning can be particularly helpful when it comes to ensuring effective assessment.
- **Medium-term planning:** includes the sort of information contained in long-term planning but broken down into more detail. It will probably cover a term, a half term or a block of time (such as six weeks). The level of detail will imply much more about the activities to be covered but probably not include individual lesson plans. This kind of detail is the sort of information to be found in the Qualifications and Curriculum Authority (QCA) schemes of work.
- **Short-term planning:** is principally lesson planning. The level of detail is much greater and starts to be related much more closely to individual classes and individual students (addressing individual needs through differentiation). Thus the lesson plan for two Year 8 classes in the same school may be similar but have subtle differences. Lesson plans will reflect the resources and accommodation available in a particular school.

A scheme of work is most commonly a long-term plan. It may contain elements of medium-term planning but will probably not contain lesson plans.

Planning is important. A few exceptional teachers seem to be able to teach very effectively with very little overt planning. For most of us the planning process helps us to reflect on and improve what we are doing. It helps if our work is set out logically and undergoes some kind of regular review process. Schemes of work are equally useful for:

■ Key Stage 3 teaching
■ examination courses
■ instrumental teaching.

An examination syllabus (GCSE, post-16 or instrumental) is not a scheme of work, although it will provide valuable information that can be incorporated into it.

Including a scheme as part of a policy

A scheme of work can be incorporated into a policy document or departmental handbook. This will define the policy and practice of a subject, department or a cross-curricular course, reflecting the school's aims and objectives. This kind of policy or handbook is a working document for the day-to-day guidance of teachers and should:

■ include aims for teaching the subject or course
■ include its objectives (derived from the aims). These might be specified in terms of knowledge, understanding, intellectual and other skills and attitudes
■ identify content in terms of skills and knowledge which students are expected to develop
■ contain guidance on:
    ■ teaching methods suitable for different aspects of work
    ■ teaching methods and differentiated work for students of different attainment levels
    ■ how work should develop from earlier experiences (including the previous phase of education)
    ■ how the progress of students should be assessed
    ■ links with other subjects/courses in the curriculum
    ■ how the subject contributes to students' spiritual, moral, social and cultural development
    ■ how students access extra instrumental tuition

- the contribution of music to literacy, numeracy (or other whole-school priorities)
- resources available in the department and how these may best be used.

A policy may address all levels of planning and it is often helpful to divide it into short, medium and long-term. Short-term planning is often easiest to tackle. It is more immediate, is needed in order to deliver next week's lessons and can often be planned on a more ad hoc basis (for example *next term's lessons can be planned next term rather than now*). However the most successful planning often leaves the short-term planning until last and starts with the long-term planning. This provides the broader picture, a framework for other planning and ensures that there is continuity and progression in learning.

Although all levels of planning are required it is important to make long-term planning a priority. This principle applies equally to Key Stage 3, examination courses and instrumental teaching. This long-term planning will constitute the departmental scheme of work, although it may be contained in a more detailed policy or departmental handbook.

One possible approach is to use or adapt the QCA schemes of work. The schemes have been developed in all subjects in order to facilitate planning. It shows one way of organizing a scheme and schools will feel free to use as little or as much of the scheme as they find helpful. The schemes give more detail about short- and medium-term planning than long-term. They can be supplemented as required or, alternatively, schools can continue to use their own scheme of work. Some teachers will wish to use their own tried and tested materials. If this is the case a rationale for the planning process will need to be adopted. The following paragraphs describe how this might be done.

How might we start this process?

We will start with long-term planning and then work down to some short-term issues. We might begin by brainstorming Key Stage 3. To begin we could write down ideas about the things to cover in each year group:

Example 1

Year 7	Year 8	Year 9
Term 1 Notation, rhythm patterns, Christmas carols	**Term 1** Keyboards, write a melody	**Term 1** Guitars
Term 2 Indian music, raps	**Term 2** Riffs, the orchestra	**Term 2** African music, Bali
Term 3 Classical music	**Term 3** Baroque music	**Term 3** The blues, pop music

The advantage of this process is that it gives a quick and easy overview of the curriculum. Reviewing our work we might, for example, decide to move keyboards from Year 8 Term 1 to Year 7 Term 3 because it will be helpful for students to have acquired these skills at an earlier age.

The disadvantages of this planning

■ how is it possible to ensure progression across the Key Stage, other than the fact that the students will have had different experiences in different years?
■ we know very little about what students will know, understand or be able to do at the end of each term and therefore lack clarity over what will be the focus for any assessments we make
■ how can we ensure that there is an effective interface between Year 6 and Year 7 (so that students feel challenged and motivated by the change over period)? One solution to this problem might be for Key Stage 3 teachers to include in their scheme information from Levels 3 and 4 of the QCA level descriptions. This will serve as a reminder of the sort of level that students will be expected to work at in the first half term of Year 7.

Improving this planning

Firstly it may be helpful to break down the statements into **intended outcomes** rather than **activities**. One way to do this is to divide statements up into knowledge, skills and understanding. For example:

Example 2

Year 7 Term 1	
By the end of the first half term students should:	By the end of the second half term students should:
Know: the terms *rhythm*, *pulse* and *time signature*.	**Know**: the structure of traditional carols, for example *verse* and *chorus*.
Understand: these terms by being to compose and listen with able understanding to pieces which use different time signatures and tempi.	**Understand**: some of the ways that words are set to music, for example *use of melisma, vocal range* and be able to demonstrate the use of some of these through composing simple carols and recognizing these features in recordings.
Skills (be able to): control rhythms, adjust tempi and be aware of the main beats of a bar in pieces using three and four beats.	**Skills (be able to)**: play a simple chord sequence on a range of tuned percussion instruments (using at least two beaters with correct technique and control).

This has some distinct advantages:

■ example 2 is easier to assess than example 1 because it gives a clearer indication of the sort of level the teacher is aiming for
■ it is easier to track progression across the term because of the emphasis on knowledge, skills and understanding
■ once this scheme is put into place lesson activities can be varied to meet the needs and interests of particular teachers, classes or students (whilst still maintaining the same intended outcomes). For example *two teachers could use different activities to teach Year 7 classes whilst still working towards the intended learning outcomes.*

It is particularly helpful if any broad overview can start with the expectations for what students will know, understand and be able to do by the end of Key Stage 3. The end of Key Stage level descriptions provides this. Curriculum planning can then work backwards from this point and ensure that students are at the appropriate level by this stage. This type of planning can give a clear sense of progression between year groups.

We might want to take this process one stage further. One way to do this is to divide the curriculum up into musical elements and then assign a particular element to each half term:

Example 3

Year 7	Year 8	Year 9
Autumn term	**Autumn term**	**Autumn term**
Duration	Duration	Duration
Pitch	Pitch	Pitch
Spring term	**Spring term**	**Spring term**
Dynamics	Dynamics	Dynamics
Tempo	Tempo	Tempo
Summer term	**Summer term**	**Summer term**
Timbre	Timbre	Timbre
Texture	Texture	Texture

(N.B. It has been assumed that the element 'structure' will be addressed in all of these.)

The order is planned so those elements that will require more time appear in the longer autumn and summer terms, whilst dynamics and tempo are put into the shorter spring term.

This kind of planning is based on the theoretical work of Bruner (1966). It assumes a spiral curriculum model where ideas and concepts are re-visited each year at a higher level, rather than a linear model which has informed much of the development of the English National Curriculum.

This model has been translated into practice as part of the Manhattanville Music Curriculum Program (1970). In this model musical concepts are developed according to a spiral planning cycle:

Example 4

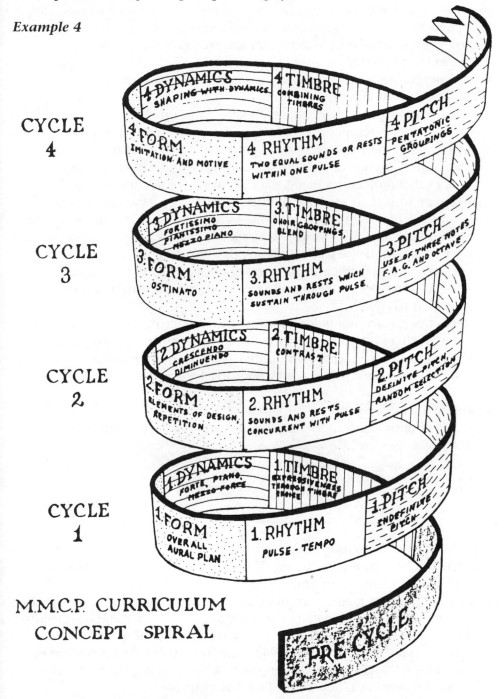

CYCLE 4

CYCLE 3

CYCLE 2

CYCLE 1

M.M.C.P. CURRICULUM
CONCEPT SPIRAL

This method of planning does have one potential disadvantage. If classroom activities concentrate solely on one element and ignore opportunities to explore others, the process can become unsatisfactory. For example: *Year 7 students are working on a project based on dynamics and are asked to compose a piece with a loud section and then a quiet section. They discuss some issues relating to techniques for controlling the dynamics of instruments and what effect this has on the music. They listen to some pieces of music from various styles and cultures noting the use of dynamic contrast and what is particularly effective.*

In this example students have prepared and understood well the concept of dynamics and dynamic contrast. However, if the students focus too much on dynamics and do not make sufficient use of other concepts such as chords, or have sufficient performing skills to make a success of this project, problems may occur. The students will need to incorporate into their work all the things that they have already learned about music. For example *although the focus for the project is dynamics they will be expected to include chords, melody and call/response (which they covered in previous topics).* If the teacher adopts this planning method he or she needs to ensure that the project is timed correctly so that students have sufficient knowledge, understanding and skills, **which they are then encouraged to use**.

Effective curriculum planning using musical elements can, if done well, ensure that there is a sense of progression in the curriculum and that particular musical concepts are not missed out or unduly neglected. It provides a framework within which to work. For example:

Example 5
Students develop their understanding of dynamics at different levels in different year groups:

Year 7: effective use of loud and quiet
Year 8: use of crescendo and diminuendo
Year 9: use of accents

This helps to give a sense of progression and the focus on dynamics means that the teacher can review the previous year's work at the start of the project. This type of incremental planning (i.e. students cover more of something in subsequent years, or at a higher/more complex level) should be tempered by the requirement for increasing quality. Greater complexity, or doing more of something, may not mean higher quality.

In this type of planning model the teacher divides the curriculum up into half-term 'blocks', tracks progression between year groups and tries to integrate activities as much as possible. For example:

Example 6

Long-term planning (Year 9 Autumn term – second half term 'Blues')
Although the teacher has decided to use the blues style as a feature of this project her planning is based on the musical elements. For this reason she places the project into a topic on pitch. This has the advantage of shifting the focus away from just engaging the class in activities within a blues idiom. As a result greater emphasis is given to the knowledge, skills and understanding she wants the students to have gained. In this example she wishes the students to be able to:

Know:
■ chords I, IV and V in C major, G major, A minor and E minor
■ the blues scale and the use of transposition to fit a new key
■ the use of sevenths and ninth chords.

Understand:
■ how to construct a chord sequence using chords I IV and V in C major, G major, A minor and E minor (including the use of two or more 12-bar blues sequences)
■ be able to recognize chords with sevenths and ninths in a range of music from different periods and styles.

Be able to:
■ play chords in specified keys and add sevenths and ninths as required, using keyboards or other tuned instruments (chords use left hand keyboard shapes rather than single finger chord function)
■ play a blues scale in specified keys and improvise a call and response idea.

Additionally:
■ begin to appreciate and possibly value musical performers from a range of musical styles.

This falls into another learning outcome category, which we might describe as *attitudes*. It is very important. The teacher decides not to formally assess this outcome. However she hopes that participating in this project will help students to:

■ value music from a wider range of styles and cultures (in this case examples of three, or more, styles of blues-influenced music)
■ see and hear black musicians performing to a high standard and present this as a positive role model
■ appreciate some of the ways that music can reflect a particular time or place.

In practice these aims may need some moderation. They provide a useful framework for assessment but there are too many statements. The teacher therefore reduces the expectations for most students and plans three levels of outcome:

- at expectation
- working towards expectation
- working above expectation.

BLUES PROJECT	
NAME:	
I know the names of the notes in chords I IV and V in C major G major A minor E minor	
I know the notes of the 'blues scale' in C major and how to transpose it to fit a new key	
I know how to add sevenths and ninths to these chords	
I have made a chord sequence using chords I IV and V in C major G major A minor E minor I have used a standard 12-bar blues sequence I have used a modified 12-bar blues sequence	

I have listened to one piece of music with sevenths and ninths in	
I have listened to two pieces of music with sevenths and ninths in	
I have listened to three pieces of music with sevenths and ninths in	
I can play chords in	
C major	
G major	
A minor	
E minor	
I can add sevenths and ninths as required	
I play chords with left hand keyboard shapes (rather than single finger chord function)	
I can play a blues scale in	
C major	
G major	
A minor	
E minor	
I can improvise a call and response idea	

For this project, in this school the teacher sets the minimum requirement for working at expectation. This is represented by the shaded text. Students who are not able to achieve this will be working towards expectation and any who are able to show evidence of being able to successfully complete all the statements will be working beyond expectation.

Self-assessment
The students are encouraged to assess their own work. They help each other to assess their work. This process helps their learning. The teacher

moderates the process and will ask students to demonstrate their ability to meet these statements. This is sometimes done in front of the whole class, sometimes in groups and sometimes with individuals. Students with special educational needs are given specific targets to work on. Those receiving help from a learning support assistant focus on these targets with the extra support provided.

The right hand column is used to:

- note the date and activity when a target was achieved
- encourage the students to make notes on information provided by the teacher
- allow the teacher to write formative comments
- allow the teacher to set and adjust future targets.

Medium-term plans

Having decided on this level of long-term planning the teacher begins to sketch out some medium-term plans. There are 28 students in a mixed ability class. Students receive one 60-minute lesson each week.

Lesson 1	1. Teacher introduction to topic. This draws on information and skills used before. For example *students are already familiar with the concept of chords and how to construct them from a given starting note.* 2. The class sings a blues song. The teacher works on singing technique in order to improve their sound. 3. All students use keyboards to practise changing chords fluently. They concentrate on the technique needed to achieve this and change chords or transpose when they are secure. 4. Students are asked to play a chord sequence to the rest of the class and discuss some of the technical difficulties and how they might overcome them. The teacher checks that the students understand how chords are constructed and how to transpose them.
Lesson 2	1. The class sing through a blues song and add some riffs. 2. The students listen to three pieces of music using chords I, IV and V. ■ an early blues piece by Muddy Waters ■ a traditional jazz band ■ a piece by Status Quo. 3. The teacher asks the students to write down what they can hear, asking them to focus on the chord sequence. Most can hear that the pieces use the same chords they practised last week. Four students know that this sequence is a 12-bar blues sequence and the teacher discusses with the class what this means. 4. The teacher picks up that one guitarist is familiar with the blues scale and introduces this idea to the class.

	5. The students are asked to improvise around a blues scale using a call and response idea. Some students can transpose this scale quite fluently. Students who receive extra instrumental lessons use their instruments for this part of the lesson.
Lesson 3	1. The class sing through the blues song. The teacher asks them what they notice about the piece. A few notice that the song is a 12-bar blues. The teacher asks about the chords which are used. She plays some of the chords with added sevenths to see if any notice that there is something different about them. A few do and the teacher discusses with the class how to add sevenths to a chord. 2. The students return to keyboards and play through a 12-bar blues sequence using seventh chords. A few begin to add improvised ideas using the blues scale.
Lesson 4	1. The class sing through the blues song. Some students are invited to add improvised riffs. 2. The teacher reminds students of the structure and checks for their understanding of the work covered so far. 3. The students are given the rest of the lesson to develop their own pieces. They have to use a blues chord sequence, added sevenths and a call and response melodic improvisation.
Lesson 5	1. The students start work straight away on their pieces. A few complete theirs and the teacher asks them to try transposing them. All groups have to perform at the end of the lesson and each group is given a target to work on next lesson.
Lesson 6	1. The groups are reminded of their target and begin work. Some adjust their chord sequence from a standard 12-bar blues to a later style. They research this information using a CD-ROM and the Internet. All groups perform at the end of the lesson and are set a target for the next lesson. 2. The class sings a blues song and focuses on stylistic devices such as bending the pitch of certain notes in order to add a blues 'feel' to the piece.

Lesson 7	1. After a brief rehearsal students record and evaluate their work. They do this using cards they were given at the start of the project. This includes statements such as:
	   ■ 'I know how to work out a chord from a given starting note'
	   ■ 'I can play fluently the chords of C, F and G'
	   ■ 'I can name three performers who use the blues style and talk about some of the differences between them' (these relate to the intended outcomes the teacher had identified in her medium-term planning).

2. Finally the teacher gives the students a brief written test, an evaluation of their composition and asks them to listen to, and evaluate, three more pieces of blues music.

Note that in this form of planning:

■ the teacher can adjust the blues song used by different classes or from year to year, whilst still working towards the same intended learning outcomes

■ the activities are designed to promote gains in skills and understanding

■ composing is treated as an activity which will help students to develop skills and understanding. Compositions are not assessed at the end of the project but the focus is put on what students can demonstrate they understand and can do. This is an important point and may result in a group or individual not achieving a completed composition but gaining high marks in demonstrating their understanding of chords, sevenths or whatever particular focus is given to the task

■ the assessment process is relatively easy because the teacher has been clear about the intended outcomes

■ all activities are integrated in a seamless and meaningful way. Singing and listening examples are related directly to students' own compositions.

The next level of detail, which would not be expected in a scheme of work, is individual lesson planning.

Other ways of planning

There are other ways to organize planning. For example, another teacher working on the same blues project may decide to set out their information in a format which mirrors the National Curriculum orders. The underlying planning remains the same but the documentation produced for the scheme of work will look different:

	Students should be taught to	By the end of this project students should be able to
Controlling sounds through singing and playing – performing skills		■ use a standard 12-bar blues sequence ■ use a modified 12-bar blues sequence

		▓ play chords in: C major G major A minor E minor ■ add sevenths and ninths as required ■ play chords with left hand keyboard shapes (rather than single finger chord function) play a blues scale in C major G major A minor E minor.
Creating and developing musical ideas – composing skills		▓ improvise a call and response idea ■ make a chord sequence using chords I, IV and V in C major G major A minor E minor.
Responding and reviewing – appraising skills		▓ have listened to and recognized the use of sevenths and ninths in two pieces of music ■ have listened to and recognized the use of sevenths and ninths in three pieces of music.

Listening, and applying knowledge and understanding		<ul><li>know the names of the notes in chords I, IV and V in</li></ul>C major G major A minor E minor <ul><li>know the notes of the 'blues scale' in C major and how to transpose it to fit a new key</li><li>know how to add sevenths and ninths to these chords.</li></ul>

The shaded statements once again represent the minimum which the teacher would expect in order for the student to be at expectation. The teacher could produce a similar 'I can do' checklist for the students to complete during and at the end of the project.

Schemes of work for examination courses

An examination course specification often gives a lot of information that can be used for planning a scheme of work. This needs to be used imaginatively. The listening section of the GCSE examination often contains useful information about musical material which students may encounter in the terminal listening examination. For example:

Pitch	Including scales, modes, intervals
Duration	Rhythms, simple and complex
Dynamics	Differences in volume, changes in volume, accents, articulation
Tempo	Differences in speed, changes in speed
Timbre	Including instrumental sounds, ways in which sound is changed, different qualities of sound

Texture	Density of instrumentation, harmony, polyphony, homophony
Structure	Patterns (for example sequence), phrasing, single idea forms (for example rounds), repetitive forms (for example pop song), developmental forms (for example variation)

Although set out within the listening section of the examination these provide ideal stimulus material for **composing** activities (see chapter 8 for more information). This approach can lead to some very good examples of integrating activities and can have a positive effect on learning.

A level specifications contain similar helpful information. Once again extracts form a historical study topic might provide material which can be used to begin planning the A level scheme of work. This might involve exploring musical ideas through composing in order to deepen knowledge and understanding of historical contexts:

■ theme and variations
■ the tonal language of music between 1700 and 1830
■ common procedures in jazz and popular music between 1920 and 1960
■ the sounds of a classical symphony orchestra
■ chord voicing
■ texture
■ figurations.

Summary points:
There are many ways of constructing a scheme of work. Successful schemes are likely to have some key features:
■ addressing long-term planning before more detailed lesson plans
■ ensuring progression across a year group and Key Stage
■ defining key learning outcomes which can be used for summative assessment
■ being practical, usable and relating to classroom practice.

Making assessment manageable and effective

Aim: this chapter sets out an overview of assessment before exploring ideas in more detail. It has relevance for all class based music teachers and instrumental teachers working both inside and outside school settings.

Introduction

Assessment can sometimes appear to be problematic in any subject – even English, mathematics and science. There are however some aspects of assessment where music has a long tradition and most people feel reasonably comfortable:

- marking GCSE or A level coursework
- instrumental/vocal examinations
- music competitions.

There are really three questions to resolve then:

1. Is assessment more difficult in music than in other subjects?
2. Why does assessment sometimes seem difficult?
3. Can we transfer aspects of assessment in music where we feel comfortable to areas where we feel less confident?

1. Is assessment more difficult in music than in other subjects?

It is not uncommon to hear comments such as:

- 'It is difficult to assess compositions.'

■ 'Assessing music is a subjective thing and you can not be objective about it.'
■ 'Aesthetic education is to do with feelings. You can not assess these.'

There is certainly something in these views. Let us examine them more closely.

Why is it that the assessment of compositions seems to be difficult? For example *when assessing compositions:*

■ *should we consider originality – and if so how do you assess this?*
■ *should we take into account the complexity of the composition?*
■ *what if the composition is the work of more than one student?*

The assessment of the GCSE composition component may help to answer some of these questions. Many early fears about how to assess GCSE compositions have been resolved. Most teachers seem to feel that they can assess pieces reasonably confidently. One of the reasons for this may be that examination boards publish clear assessment criteria. Following these criteria helps the teacher to feel comfortable. It may be helpful therefore to have some similar criteria when we assess compositions at Key Stage 3.

Activities and outcomes

Composing is an activity not an outcome. This is a very important distinction and a source of much confusion. A helpful way of thinking about this may be to consider the difference between the **activity** (composing) and the **outcome** (composition). They are not the same thing. For example *students might be working on a composition based on added sevenths and can demonstrate their understanding of this concept because they are able to play these chords individually, or in pairs.* Thus the **activity** (composing) shows their understanding and is relatively straightforward to assess: students can play and use chords with added sevenths, they can do this fluently or they are working towards this skill.

The **outcome** (the composition) is a different matter. Once we start to consider the composition as an outcome (which therefore requires assessment) we will need to make judgements about:

■ the structure of the piece
■ how effective it is
■ the technical skills used.

We will also need to make judgements about a range of other things which can make the whole thing seem more complex and difficult to manage. One way to avoid this problem is to consider that, on some occasions, it may be helpful not to assess the **composition**, but to focus on the skills and understanding the students demonstrate whilst **composing**. The result will be that the finished composition is actually less important than the skills that students demonstrated while they were composing. These skills will be much easier to assess than the finished composition. Finished compositions will need to be assessed from time to time. When doing so it is probably most helpful to consider them as end points in a process (i.e. outcomes) and to use GCSE-type criteria.

However, when teaching GCSE students in Years 10 and 11 it is not always helpful to only assess against the criteria supplied by examination boards. At key points the teacher will need to use these criteria (and will hopefully share them with students so that they are familiar with them). However, if this is the only type of assessment used for GCSE students there will be limitations. For example *if it is the only method used with Year 10 students*. These students may be starting to develop their confidence, and need specific targets in order to improve. The criteria used for the terminal examination may be de-motivating if used too early in the course. As we have already noted students aged 14–16 may need to engage in **composing** activities, which help their understanding, but which do not always lead to a finished **composition**. The same applies to post-16 courses. See chapters 2, 8 and 9 for further information about these points.

Following this principle we can see two types of assessment emerging:

TYPE 1

Activity ➜ e.g. *composing* ➜ teacher assesses the skills, knowledge and understanding demonstrated as students compose (but not the composition)

TYPE 2

Outcome ➜ e.g. *composition* ➜ the teacher uses specific criteria (such as those used by GCSE examination boards) to assess a composition

---

Composition and composing

If it may not always be appropriate to assess a **composition** (so much as the contribution an individual has made to the **composing** process). We might want to look for evidence of a student's ability to understand a concept (for example *a chord structure*), use it effectively and recognize similar ideas in the music of other composers. So originality, whilst it is to be applauded and nurtured wherever possible, is clearly not the most important facet of the composing activity. It is rarely helpful to include it as a specific criterion against which to assess compositions. Likewise the complexity of a composition is usually not as important as its effectiveness. Whilst it is not straightforward to assess the contribution an individual makes to a group composition, it should be possible to see how far a particular student understands a concept (for example *chords, dominant sevenths, ostinato)* through their contribution to the composing process.

Thinking about this difference between activity and outcome can therefore be very helpful. It is also beneficial when planning a scheme of work. See chapter 2 for more details.

A general principle worth remembering is that assessment is more difficult when it is added at the end of a planning process. For example *the teacher plans the curriculum and then plans how to assess it.* If the teacher decides what the students are to learn before planning the curriculum, assessment becomes relatively straightforward. For example *assessment will mean either seeing how far the students have met this aim (summative assessment) or offering students targets, written comments or verbal suggestions in order to help them to achieve the desired aim (formative assessment).*

◼ 2. Why does assessment sometimes seem difficult?

The key to effective assessment, in any subject, can often be found through greater clarity over terms and concepts. Confusion over terminology can make things seem more difficult. We have already noted that ensuring assessment comes at the start of the process and making sure we focus on the outcome (rather than the activity) can help.

There are other aspects of assessment where a confusion of terms can be unhelpful. For example there are three common processes used in assessment:

- ◼ assessment
- ◼ recording
- ◼ reporting.

Some of the confusion which arises over assessment can be removed when this terminology is used accurately.

For example *when talking about assessment it is tempting to discuss marks or grades.* This is part of the assessment process but there is more to it than this. Or *we might talk to someone about our assessment 'system' by showing them the mark sheet we use* and as a result actually end up discussing the way we **record** assessments. Once again the two are linked. They must be. However designing an elaborate system which records our marks and grades may not lead to effective assessment. Sometimes an enormous amount of time and effort is put into a system which records a great deal of information but which does not help students to learn. We want to devise a system that:

■   is clear
■   is easy to use
■   has a beneficial effect on learning
■   does not take up enormous amounts of time.

Similarly, although most people will be familiar with the terms 'formative' and 'summative' assessment, a lack of clarity over practice can lead to confusion, or even shortcomings. We will return to look at these terms in more detail later.

■ 3. Can we transfer aspects of assessment in music where we feel comfortable to areas where we feel less confident?

We have noted that some aspects of music education have built up a strong tradition of assessment methodology. Graded instrumental/vocal examinations provide a good example of an area of music education where assessments are regularly made and where a certain authority has grown up around the systems that are used. Clearly there are things that we can learn from this system.

There are however a number of points we will have to bear in mind:

■   assessment in instrumental/vocal examinations is principally 'summative' only (it tells you whether you have met the required standard by 'passing' and gives you an indication of how well you did compared to other candidates)
■   a lot of the assessment may be quite subjective (one examiner may give a different mark to another)
■   it often assumes a particular performance style (performing from notation in a Western classical tradition) which may be appropriate for only a small minority of students and which is therefore not going to have relevance for other students.

This kind of system therefore has relevance for a few students but can not be applied to all without considerable modification. It will probably only apply to the assessment of performing and not to composing or appraising music.

Having given an overview, let us now examine some of these points in more detail.

Why do we assess?

It may be helpful to remind ourselves of the reasons why we want to assess, so we are working from important principles. If there were no reason to assess we could dispense with the whole process immediately. However, teachers realize that assessment is important and often devote large amounts of time and effort to it. They want to get it right and feel that their efforts are worthwhile. Investment in planning effective and manageable assessment can save time in the long run and make life less stressful.

We assess in order to:

1. Gain accurate information on the development, progress and achievement of students. This sort of information is required in order to give information to parents. For example *reports*. Parents will want to know:
    - where their child is in relation to the attainment of his or her peers and what might be expected for their age group
    - how much effort their child has been putting into his or her work
    - how much progress their child has made since the last feedback.
    - what their child needs to do in order to make progress.
2. Evaluate the teaching and learning which has taken place, in order to see how effective a project has been and whether it should be adjusted in the future or whether particular students need to develop some specific skills.
3. Increase motivation and individual responsibility for learning (when students are clear about what they are doing, why they are doing it and what they need to do in order to improve, they often feel motivated).

If, however, the assessment process seems to have run out of control and to have taken over what we are doing, adjustments may need to be made. Unless it is helping the teacher, student or parent to improve performance it can become a pointless activity. We never want to reach the situation where we are so busy assessing that we no longer teach effectively and students stop learning.

◼ Assessment, recording and reporting

We have already noted that assessment, recording and reporting are closely linked and can easily be confused. For example *we may start our work on assessment planning by drawing up assessment forms*. Before doing this we perhaps need to ask:

- what it is we are trying to assess
- how we intend to go about it.

Careful consideration of whether we are dealing with assessment, recording or reporting can clarify issues in a helpful way.

Assessment

Assessment is the process by which the teacher (or student) makes judgements about teaching and learning within music lessons. There are four common types of assessment activity:

1. Giving marks or grades. This is usually summative. For example *students are given a mark for attainment or effort (usually towards the end of a project)*.
2. Observation of activity in order to try and assess understanding. This is usually formative. For example *the teacher observes students as they are working in groups and notes individual differences, areas needing improvement and assesses how effective teaching has been.*
3. Question and answer techniques used to elicit understanding. This is usually formative. For example *at the end of a lesson the teacher asks a group of students to play back their compositions. He or she also asks other students questions about what works well, what they can hear and how work might be improved still further.*
4. Making comments to students about targets for improvement. This is usually formative. For example *during the course of a lesson, or a project, the teacher notes those areas of a student's work that require specific improvement and discusses with the student how this might be achieved and what sort of target would be appropriate to aim for.*

All assessment types are relevant in music education and a balance of these techniques will give secure information for planning future work. Most schools have a policy on these areas and it is helpful if the techniques used for assessment match what is happening in other subjects. A common approach will help students to understand how their work is assessed throughout the school.

What might we find in a music lesson where these techniques are working effectively?

- students' work is regularly evaluated (probably once every half term)
- the criteria for these evaluations are clear (to the teacher, students and parents)

- the criteria used are consistently applied
- students are encouraged to use assessments as indications of how to make improvements in their work. For example *they are given information about what they are expected to know, understand and be able to do as part of a project. During the project, and more formally at the end of the project, they evaluate their work (with the help of the teacher)*
- there is evidence in the teacher's planning of a response to individual students (differentiation).

As noted earlier this process can be much more difficult when:

- we try to assess **activities**, rather than **outcomes**
- assessment is grafted on to the end of planning (rather than being the starting point).

Recording

Once assessments are made they need to be recorded so that they can be used for future reference. The emphasis should be on 'knows and understands' (outcomes) rather than 'has done' (activity). Accurate records give secure information, which can be used for the purposes of report writing.

Over-emphasis on the method used for recording information can lead to ineffective and time-consuming assessment.

Reporting

Our expectations for report writing have moved a long way in the last decade and the standard of report writing has improved greatly.

Once a year, teachers are required to give a report to parents on a student's progress in all subjects. At key points the report will contain information on the National Curriculum level descriptions (for example *for students aged 14*). These are essentially summative statements about students' work. They should also describe the progress that has been made since the last report.

Ideally students should be made aware of the methods used to assess their work and should be encouraged to become involved in the appraisal of their own work.

What is the difference between formative and summative assessment?

The terms 'formative' and 'summative' assessment have already been used and are probably familiar. Despite this, it is still not uncommon to find assessment criteria in music departments which are predominantly summative in nature. Once again, clarity in terminology and application can be very helpful.

Summative assessments provide teachers, students and parents with information about the stage a particular student has reached at a specified time. We have already noted that instrumental graded examinations are one example of assessment with a strong summative element. This is the mark or grade given (the comments made will often be more formative in nature and may give information about how the student can improve). Usually summative assessment information is related to peer group, age-related expectations or a particular grade or mark.

A common form of summative assessment might be found in an end of year report. The student is given a grade and a comment.

Name John Brown
Class 7d
Attainment B
Effort 2

Plus the comment:

John has worked well this year and I was pleased with the work that he did on chords during the project on reggae.

The students and the parents know how John has done in terms of attainment. He seems to have done better than average (because the school uses a grading system which goes from A–E and John has scored a B). John has also got quite a good grade for effort. The effort grade may mean that he has quite a good attitude in the lessons. These grades are summative. The report also includes a comment, which gives some formative information. However, although we know the teacher was pleased with a particular topic we do not know what John needs to do in order to improve and get A for attainment and 1 for effort in Year 8. The report therefore lacks formative content. Nor do we have much information about the progress that John has made.

There are two important points which need to be considered:

1. If the teacher has been making a series of formative assessments during the year and John already knows what was good about the reggae project and how he can improve, the information provided on the report is perfectly adequate. John will be receiving formative comments as part of regular assessment in lessons. If, however, the teacher has made some assessments of John's work during the year but not shared

them, and the first John knew about the teacher's views was when he received the report, there is scope for improving the communication between teacher and student. If the teacher has not thought about this until writing the reports, there is considerable scope for improvement.

2. If the student or parent were to ask the teacher how a decision had been reached to award a grade B for attainment, would the teacher be able to show the evidence which had led to the decision? Did John Brown get a grade B because, over a period of time it was the average grade that he was awarded for various projects, and so a grade B would be about what he might expect? Or has the teacher given a quite subjective grade, based on a number of factors that are a little hard to define?

Even less helpful are reports that comment mainly on attitudes:

> **Julian White**
> **Attainment** C
> **Effort** 1

> *I have been pleased with some of the work that Julian has done this year. He is a conscientious student and has a good attitude to his work.*

The report gives little information about what Julian has done, what he was good at and how he can improve.

It lacks formative assessment, which gives information about what it is that the student will need to do in order to improve and do better. Julian would like to move from a grade C to B or A. However, it is hard for him to improve without clear information about what needs to be done. Over-concentration on summative assessment can therefore be de-motivating for students. It can also lead teachers to think that assessment is pointless and appears to be taking them away from the task of teaching.

Formative assessment

Formative assessment is more diagnostic and gives information to teachers, students and parents about how a student is progressing and which areas need to be improved. It can help to motivate students.

Formative assessment consists of:

- comments made by the teacher to the student about how to improve a particular aspect of their work
- written comments on a piece of work which give information about how work could develop and improve

- diagnostic comments on a report which enable a student to improve their work.

Formative verbal comments:

Example 1

> *A Year 10 student is working on a composition based on modes. The teacher asks the student to evaluate his work. The student says that the piece sounds muddled and that he is finding it difficult to make progress. The teacher suggests that the student has so much musical material that achieving structure and coherence is difficult. The teacher suggests that the student should isolate two or three ideas and try to develop them more fully, in order to gain more coherence.*

Formative written comments:

Example 2

> *A Year 12 student is harmonizing a chorale type melody. The teacher does not give a mark for the work but writes detailed comments about the use of consecutive fifths and part writing. The next time the student tackles a similar exercise there is evidence of some improvement.*

Involving students in self-assessment

With careful planning and management the involvement of students in assessment can have a significant impact on motivation and the quality of work produced. It is clearly important that the students have an understanding of **what** they are doing and **how** they are doing. Some activities are not appropriate for self-assessment and the teacher will need to use discretion. However self-assessment should be encouraged because:

- it can improve motivation
- it can lead to better communication between the teacher and student
- it can provide the teacher with useful insights into how a student perceives an activity
- it can enhance the validity of teacher assessment.

A weakness of self-assessment is that students are sometimes asked to evaluate in an unfocused and uninformed way:

Example 3

> *I liked it when we played the drums in the piece with a drone because we had a good beat.*

The teacher has gained information about the students' attitudes. It is useful to know that the students enjoyed the project, but the information will not really help the students to achieve higher standards and the records of the students' own assessments will not help the teacher when writing reports.

The problem with this assessment has arisen due to a lack of communication between the teacher and the students. The teacher needs to:

- have clear identified learning outcomes
- have shared with the students an appropriate way to assess their work
- discussed with the students ways in which their work could be improved.

Other ways of involving students in summative assessment

At the end of the project the teacher might decide that he wishes to make a final assessment of the students' work. It is once again important to give clear information about how the work is to be assessed. The teacher may say for example that the compositions are going to be assessed using grades A–E for attainment and that in addition each group, or each individual, will receive an effort grade of 1–5. This information is useful for the students and they might be asked to make an assessment of the grade they think they should be given.

Perhaps even more useful would be for the teacher to try and give some kind of criteria to go with the grades. For example *when working on a project which focuses on semitones and chord clusters students could be asked to assess themselves using the following criteria:*

a. *In this project I made effective use of semitones and clusters and it is imaginative and interesting.*
b. *In this project I made effective use of both semitones and clusters.*
c. *In this project I made some use of semitones and clusters.*
d. *In this project I made some use of either semitones or clusters.*
e. *In this project I did not make use of semitones or clusters.*

In practice there may be too many statements. Most projects will probably only require three. They will probably describe:

- the expectation (achieved by the majority of students)
- attainment above expectation
- working towards the expectation.

See chapter 2 for further information.

Criteria can easily be devised for effort and these will probably be applicable to most projects.

By the time end-of-year reports come to be written the teacher might have records of a number of effective self-assessments. The advantages for the teacher are:

■ students should understand the criteria used for reaching decisions about these assessments
■ the teacher's records will provide secure information, which can be used for report writing, and the students will understand any comments that are made (since they themselves were actively involved in the assessment procedure).

The key to making this successful will be the criteria that are given to students for their self-assessment. If they are too open-ended they are unlikely to be successful.

◼ What are learning outcomes in music and how should I plan for them?

Learning outcomes are what a teacher expects students to achieve as a result of engaging in some form of musical activity. A curriculum that does not define learning outcomes and plan for assessment against them risks becoming haphazard and flawed. Refer to chapter 2 for more information. We have already noted that it is preferable to plan these **before** the activities that are intended to achieve them. So what do learning outcomes look like?

They are commonly expressed in terms of knowledge, skills, attitudes and understanding.

Attitudes

Attitudes are important. For example *it is pointless planning a curriculum if students end up disliking music at the end of it.* Attitudes are relatively easy to assess since all the teacher has to do is ask the student for information about their attitudes to a particular topic:

For example *in a Year 8 class students have been working on syncopation. The teacher informally questions the students about their attitudes to ragtime music. A student says:*

'I liked the bit we did on ragtime and I thought that the way Scott Joplin used syncopation in his pieces was really effective.'

The teacher knows that the student has listened to the music of Scott Joplin, appreciated one of its distinctive characteristics and valued the style of the music.

Knowledge

Knowledge in music is facts about pieces, people or things. Facts (and therefore knowledge) are easy to assess:

■ how many symphonies did Beethoven write?
■ how many strings are there on a violin?
■ what notes are they tuned to?
■ rearrange these letters into an instrument: TARIS.

Although they are easy to assess, facts are a potential pitfall within the music curriculum. Teaching facts can result in time consuming and peripheral activity. Students will usually fill in missing words or complete worksheets quite happily. Answering questions in this way can appear to give music credibility and put it on a par with other 'academic' subjects. A danger arises from putting activities into the music curriculum because they are easy and manageable to assess. Assessment is driving the curriculum, rather than serving it.

The teacher may wish students to acquire a particular piece of knowledge and may want them to know certain facts about music or musicians. However, he needs to be aware of the dangers of constructing a curriculum based around knowledge. For example *when planning lessons on Danse Macabre by Saint Saens. The lessons consist only of writing information about the composer, the piece of music and then listening to it.* The project may contain a lot of activity, but it is divorced from the students' own practical exploration of music. Knowledge about music has been allowed to replace understanding of music.

Understanding

Understanding is harder to define and therefore harder to assess. It is however fundamental to what we are trying to achieve as music teachers.

In the example quoted above we mentioned Danse Macabre as an example of a piece which is often written about in music lessons (quite often at all Key Stages!) What are the features of the piece that we wish to concentrate on with the students? It can be useful to refer to the musical elements contained within the National Curriculum orders for music.

The teacher might decide to start by looking at timbre and decide to pose some questions to the students:

■ which instruments can be used to create a 'spooky' atmosphere?
■ what special effects can we get from the instruments that we have available in order to enhance the effect we want to create?

The teacher may wish to move on to some of the other musical elements. Eventually the students will be equipped with the understanding that they need in order to explore these ideas in a composition. They might be given a plot similar to that used by Saint Saens and then asked to compose their own pieces of music.

The project should result in the students having acquired some knowledge about music. Far more importantly they may have acquired understanding about the ways that the musical elements can be used to create an atmosphere or effect, because they have explored this idea in their compositions. Once they have reached this stage it would make sense for them to look at the way that Saint Saens dealt with the same idea and compare their own work with his. They should hear the piece with some understanding of the processes involved in composing it.

Assessing understanding

Understanding can be assessed through:

1. Listening to compositions to see how effective students have been in using the musical material they are working with and whether they have managed to create the desired effect.
2. Asking them questions whilst they are composing or rehearsing pieces of music.
3. Asking them about what processes they can hear going on in a piece of music they listen to. Their answers will give good information about the level of their musical understanding.

These procedures require the teacher to be astute and to make effective use of questioning.

Skills

Students will need to develop skills in each Key Stage. These will include:

- performing pieces on an instrument/voice
- developing a sense of ensemble
- ICT skills
- improvisation skills
- playing by ear and from memory
- the ability to develop and extend compositions
- being able to communicate with an audience
- working together in a group
- presentation skills.

Some skills are relatively easy to assess. For example *information on summative performance assessments can be found in examination specifications and instrumental examination schemes*. There is a long tradition of assessing these skills. Others are less regularly assessed. For example *working together in a group or presentation skills*. More thought may need to be given about how to assess these. Clarity over the intended outcome should make assessment in all these areas possible. These outcomes can be shared with students, they can be asked to make their own self-assessments and helpful verbal and written formative comments can be given.

Using the National Curriculum level descriptions for Key Stage 3 students

Towards the end of Year 9, students will need to be assessed against the National Curriculum level descriptions. This will be a summative assessment and will be based on information that has been obtained and recorded about what a student knows, understands and can do (i.e. learning outcomes). Because the level description is a summative assessment it is probably not helpful to plan your assessment system around it. This is a similar point to the one already made about not necessarily using terminal examination criteria with students during the early part of their course. For example *it may be helpful to put into place an assessment system which is mostly related to your scheme of work and then to assess against the level descriptions at the end of Year 9.*

Provided your scheme of work addresses the National Curriculum programme of study this should not pose too many problems. For example *during Years 7–9 students will control sounds through singing and playing, create and develop musical ideas, respond to and review music, listen to music and apply knowledge and understanding*. Therefore by the end of Year 9, students will have covered all the relevant sections of the music Key Stage 3 National Curriculum Programme of Study.

Some teachers may want to divide their assessment methodology into five strands, based on the paragraphs on pp. 20–21 in the music National Curriculum document. This is certainly a possibility. The danger of this process is that the assessment might be added on at the end, rather than being an integral part of the process. This is why careful planning of the scheme of work is so important and why it can save a lot of time and confusion when it comes to thinking about assessment.

Whichever way it is done the teacher should end up with quite a lot of information about the student:

- marks or grades in a mark book
- pieces of work that have written comments
- verbal comments that have been made to the student
- targets for improvement that have been set
- other information that the teacher knows about the student.

This information will now be used in order to inform the level that the student can best be described as working at.

Using level descriptions

Most 14-year-old students will be working at levels 5 or 6. In order to help make a decision about which level to apply, it is possible to break the statements in the level description down into their separate parts and give examples by each statement of how students have demonstrated this achievement. The students could be involved in this process themselves.

LEVEL 5 (give examples of how students have achieved this)	
Pupils identify and explore musical devices and how music reflects time and place.	
They perform significant parts from memory and from notations with awareness of their own contribution such as leading others, taking a solo part and/or providing rhythmic support.	
They improvise melodic and rhythmic material within given structures, use a variety of notations.	
They compose music for different occasions using appropriate musical devices such as melody, rhythms, chords and structures.	
They analyse and compare musical features.	
They evaluate how venue, occasion and purpose affects the way music is created, performed and heard.	
They refine and improve their work.	

LEVEL 6 (give examples of how students have achieved this)	
Pupils identify and explore the different processes and contexts of selected musical genres and styles.	
They select and make expressive use of tempo, dynamics, phrasing and timbre.	
They make subtle adjustments to fit their own part within a group performance.	
They improvise and compose in different genres and styles, using harmonic and non-harmonic devices where relevant, sustaining and developing musical ideas and achieving different intended effects.	
They use relevant notations to plan, revise and refine material.	
They analyse, compare and evaluate how music reflects the contexts in which it is created, performed and heard.	
They make improvements to their own and other's work in the light of the chosen style.	

Of course some students will be at higher or lower levels. Some of these statements could be broken down still further. For example:

LEVEL 6 (give examples of how students have achieved this)	
They improvise and compose in different genres and styles.	
Using harmonic and non-harmonic devices where relevant.	
Sustaining and developing musical ideas.	
Achieving different intended effects.	

This process is very thorough, but may end up being too cumbersome.

◼ Reviewing current assessment policy and practice

Here is a stage-by-stage plan of how to plan or review how you assess. There are nine steps.

1. Start by making sure that you have a clear scheme of work. Do not rely on a series of lessons which are not related to each other and which do not ensure a dynamic and progressive curriculum. For example *a selection of ideas taken from different books, courses or from initial teacher training.* There should be clear planning which ensures progression between year groups and across the Key Stage. In planning your curriculum you will have to think about:

    ◼ the resources available
    ◼ the expertise available
    ◼ the training needed
    ◼ delivering the National Curriculum
    ◼ achieving your school's aims and objectives
    ◼ achieving your subject aims and objectives.

2. Provided your curriculum delivers the National Curriculum Programmes of Study you should be able to relate any assessment directly to your scheme of work. Your records of any assessments made will then provide you with secure information with which to write reports and, in Year 9, to assess how successfully the students have matched the level descriptions. It should be possible for you to define your intended learning outcomes for each topic or block of work covered. A good rule of thumb is that you should have some idea of what you want to achieve with your students each half term. You might want to divide what it is that you want them to achieve into:

    ◼ knowledge
    ◼ skills
    ◼ understanding
    ◼ attitudes.

    For example:
    A Year 9 class is doing a project on the 'blues'. The class will work on the project for six one-hour lessons. They will compose pieces based on the 12-bar blues, sing blues songs and listen to a variety of pieces, which are based on the blues.

The intended learning outcomes might be:

a.   Knowledge
- know chords of C, F and G
- know notes of blues scale
- know two blues singers
- know the relationship between African pentatonic music and the blues
- know the order of chords in a 12-bar blues sequence.

b.   Skills
- be able to play chords of C, F and G on a keyboard using left hand
- be able to improvise a short 'fill' (based on blues scale) using the right hand on a keyboard
- be able to sing a short blues phrase independently
- be able to play short 'riffs' (using right hand on keyboard with at least four fingers)
- be able to use a sequencer to record performances and improvisations for future playback and analysis.

c.   Understanding
- understand the social significance of the blues for black Americans
- understand the distinctive chord structure of the blues and the effect that it creates in a piece of music
- understand the expressive qualities of the blues as demonstrated through blue notes heard in recorded performances
- understand the nature of call and response ideas in recorded performances and demonstrate this in compositions.

d.   Attitudes
- develop a positive attitude to the rich musical heritage of the blues
- enjoy experience of playing in an ensemble and improvising phrases.

These outcomes are intended as an example only and each teacher will need to define their own outcomes in the light of their scheme of work. In order to make it even more manageable you may want fewer stated outcomes. Three for each project would be ample (with the statements broken down into three levels: working towards, at expectation and working above expectation).

It would be helpful to give these statements to students at the start of the project, encourage them to constantly refer to them and to use them (with the students involved) to assess the final outcome of each project. When asking the students to refer to them you might also want to set them specific targets for improvement.

3. Decide how you are going to assess these outcomes (bearing in mind the whole school policy on assessment). Are you giving:
   - verbal comments
   - grades
   - effort grades
   - grades with criteria attached
   - marks
   - self-assessed statement banks.

   You will probably want all of these.

4. Give helpful, formative comments, which will enable the students to improve.

5. At a certain time in the project (probably the end) undertake some kind of summative assessment and give students a grade. Involve the students in this process so that they can see and understand what is happening.

6. Record the grades and any important comments on a record sheet.

7. At the end of the year use the information on your record sheet to write reports. Make sure that the report is fair and relates clearly to what the student has done. Avoid general comments about attitude unless they are particularly relevant. Concentrate on what the students have achieved.

8. At the end of Year 9, or at another appropriate time, use your records (and the records of other teachers who have taught the student) to make a judgement about the level a student is working at. Get the student to evaluate himself or herself as well so that they have a clear understanding of what they have achieved and why they have been successful or not in reaching the level of the description.

9. In the light of the information you have gathered review and refine your schemes of work.

Summary points:
- Assessment is made easier by clarity over terminology.
- It is easier if assessment aims are set out before planning the activities that will be undertaken.
- Give students information about expectations for each project, use these to set targets and keep records of how well they do. Provided this information is well focused it can be useful to involve students in a certain amount of self-assessment.

Differentiation

Aim: this chapter describes some of the ways that we can cater for students' individual learning needs.

Introduction

The word 'differentiation' has often been used in education. It was more commonly found in schools prior to the introduction of the National Curriculum. Subsequently teachers tended to concentrate more on areas raised in the National Curriculum Orders and in the OFSTED inspection framework. Neither made direct reference to the term differentiation, although both strongly implied the need for a curriculum that responds to the needs of individual students. What does the term mean?

> *'... [the curriculum] has to allow for difference in the abilities and other characteristics of children, even of the same age.'*

> (HMI 1980)

Differentiation acknowledges that within groups students will have differing experiences, capabilities and interests. The definition adopted for the purpose of this chapter is:

> *'Meeting the different needs, experiences, interests and capabilities of individual pupils within a group.'*

This means that it has relevance to all teachers regardless of whether a school is selective, mainstream comprehensive or a special school. It applies to mixed ability classes and to groups taught in sets. It also applies to the smaller groups of students taught by instrumental teachers.

◢ What are the differences we need to cater for?

Catering for differences poses several challenges. Students will have a variety of prior experiences – some gained in schools and much more that has been acquired out of school. They will have for example:

- different skill levels
- language development
- motivation
- interest
- ICT skills
- literacy skills
- levels of concentration
- levels of confidence and self-esteem.

Theoretically each student is an individual and therefore requires an individual learning programme. This is the sort of expectation we have for students with identified special needs, who are given an Individual Education Plan. In practice this is not possible for all students and compromises will need to be made. In the future new technologies may make a more individualized approach much more realistic. An example of this sort of practice can be found through computer-based Individual Learning Programmes (most often used to support core skills of numeracy and literacy). In the meantime the National Literacy and Numeracy Strategy is encouraging teachers to focus on three groups of students:

- working at expectation
- above expectation
- below expectation.

This is a quite broad approach to learning. It may not cater sufficiently for students' individual differences. For example *A student is described by a mathematics teacher as working below expectation for her age. In order to improve the attainment of this student and hopefully move her closer to expectation the teacher will need to consider why the student is below expectation. Some of this may involve analysis of the fact that she is less successful at solving algebra problems. Therefore the teacher intends to practise this skill with the student. However the teacher has not explored some of the additional factors which are leading to under-achievement. This student becomes more negative about equations the more she practises them. This is because of low self-esteem. Practising equations and being given extra homework only exacerbates the problem.*

The key here is that although identifying three levels of attainment within a class or group can be very useful, it is not the whole, or the end, of the story. An effective teacher will be planning informally and formally some strategies for teaching these groups of students. The teacher will take account of their levels of attainment but will also need to consider a range of other, sometimes complex, information as well. This will sometimes require more detailed information about individuals and how to ensure they learn effectively. In a secondary school a class music teacher will have a limited amount of contact with Key Stage 3 students. Clearly there are limitations to how well the teacher can respond to individual needs. As students move into examination courses the teacher will know them better and a more individual approach should become increasingly possible. Instrumental teachers see relatively few numbers of students and might therefore be capable of taking a more individual approach with students.

Differentiation by outcome and task

A common response to differentiation describes ways in which differing needs can be catered for. The two most common are task and outcome:

1. Differentiation by task is a method of organization used by teachers to cater for students' prior experience or attainment. For example:

    A Year 8 class is working on 'modes'. During a practical task the teacher describes three levels of activity she wants the students to achieve.
    - *Level 1 should be able to play the notes of two modes on a keyboard*
    - *Level 2 should be able to play the notes of three modes on a keyboard and two chords as an accompaniment*
    - *Level 3 should be able to play fluently the notes of three modes on a keyboard and accompany an improvisation.*

    The teacher gives all students information about these three levels. The groups are organized so that students who are experienced and working above expectation are encouraged to achieve Level 3 as their target. Less experienced students are encouraged to try to achieve Level 1.

This is an example of the way the teacher has organized the lesson so that students have a slightly different task, which is matched to their prior attainment or experience. Managed well this approach can be very effective. It requires careful planning and in most cases this would be indicated through the departmental scheme of work (i.e. medium-term planning which did not take account of particular individuals in a class or group). Similar, related strategies might involve giving slightly different resources (for example *some students use a computer and sequencer software*). This type of approach is sometimes described as differentiation by resources or group.

2. Differentiation by outcome occurs when students are set a more open-ended task and are likely to achieve differing levels. It is often mentioned as a strategy within a GCSE examination syllabus. In some contexts it can be useful. For example:

    A Year 10 class are asked to compose a piece which makes use of ninth and eleventh chords. The students have differing experiences and the work they produce reflects this.

The drawback of this strategy is that it merely gives an indication of a student's prior attainment. The more experienced students do well and the less experienced do less well. However it may not help students, particularly the less experienced, to move on in their learning. They can remain stuck. If they receive a diet of lessons that differentiate principally by outcome they are likely to make less progress than they are capable of.

Ideally a curriculum plan and individual lessons will contain a skilful mixture of approaches. Some tasks will be differentiated by task and some by outcome. Tasks will be modified in lessons in order to respond to individual students' needs and interests.

What do we want students to achieve?

In adapting our teaching to cater for students' differences we need to consider what we want them to achieve. Only if we are clear about this can we hope to achieve success. For example *what do we judge success to look like?* This question throws up some interesting points, since the answer we give will usually relate to our own experiences of music making and can be surprisingly narrow. The National Curriculum alone will not supply us with the answer. A commitment to differentiation may require us to re-think our assumptions about what we want to achieve, and therefore the way we will teach to make sure this happens successfully.

Imagine, for example, a Year 9 class and think for a moment about successful musicians in the class. They will probably have received instrumental/vocal tuition and be fluent performers. If we were to try to define a list of skills needed in order to be a successful musician what would our criteria be? They may provide useful clues about the way we need to organize our teaching.

A successful musician can:

- listen to music from a wide variety of styles and cultures
- play by ear and from notation(s)
- communicate expressively using the voice and/or an instrument
- improvise and compose fluently
- listen to music with great insight and aural acuity.

It therefore follows that a successful musician is not necessarily just someone who can:

- read music
- pass examinations using a voice or an instrument
- tell you when Mozart was born and the composition dates of his symphonies
- play or sing with technical accuracy but without expression
- play or sing in only one musical style.

Go back to our Year 9 class for a moment and consider again the question of the successful musician in the group. It is possible that those who have received the extra tuition may not meet all these criteria. It is equally possible that there will be other students who have not received formal tuition but who are very successful at what they do.

Let us illustrate the point further by considering the progress made by some students at various stages in their lives:

Darren

Started the trumpet at 14 and made rapid progress. At music college he found his teacher was more interested in practising for his own concerts and seemed to want to undermine him. He gave up and worked for the civil service. Recently he has joined a soul band and he plays regularly with them in local gigs.

Natasha

Started the flute at the age of 11. By the age of 14 her teacher had persuaded her to give up since she was not going to make the standard for the local music centre band. She sold the flute and bought a bass guitar. She met some other musicians and started playing in a band. Two years later they were spotted at a club, were recorded and made it into the national charts.

Spider

Spider plays in a Bhangra group. He is very quiet and some people find this difficult, believing him to be insolent. At school he played in a Samba band during lunch times. He twice auditioned for percussion lessons but the teacher rejected him. During a Samba workshop a visiting tutor commented that he was the most talented drummer she had ever met. He now teaches and runs workshops in a local youth club.

Anna

Anna is a Year 4 class teacher in a rural primary school. She is terrified of teaching music and classes herself as unmusical. She had no choice about taking her class for music and this year has been working on a composition project based on the 'Firebird'. Her pupils have composed pieces which they have related to the music of Stravinsky. When the school was inspected recently her music teaching was graded as excellent.

Cheryl

Cheryl plays in a folk band out of school. She can play accordion, guitar, harp and sing fluently. The music teacher is not aware of this and considers her to be slightly below average. Cheryl has decided not to continue with music beyond Year 9.

Sally

Sally has Rett syndrome. She is not expected to live past her 11th birthday. She attends a local special school where a music therapist is helping her to explore instruments. She occasionally shows some sign that she is responding.

All these students are successful musicians in many different and varied ways. At key points in their lives they have actually considered themselves, or been considered by others, musical failures. Even Sally, whom many would not readily classify as a successful musician. The reason is that the parameters by which they, or their teachers, defined success were relatively narrow and restrictive.

Catering for individual learning needs

Not everyone learns in the same way. Some people learn by:

- discovering for themselves
- instruction
- reading information
- listening to information
- working in groups
- working independently using CD-ROMs or other resources.

It is probably desirable to encourage students to consider for themselves how they learn most effectively. This might be a whole-school issue. It certainly has relevance for music lessons, including individual or small group instrumental lessons. For example, a teacher is working with a Year 8 class on a traditional spiritual. A conventional teaching approach might be as follows:

1. Teacher hands out the words.
2. Teacher sings the song (breaking it down into small sections).
3. Class sing by responding as directed.
4. Teacher gets small group of students to add a simple rhythmic accompaniment.
5. Students copy out part of the melody onto a piece of manuscript paper.
6. Students copy out some information about the historical and cultural background of spirituals.

This represents a sound but relatively narrow range of learning opportunities for the students. Another teacher might:

1. Play the melody line and consider with students the implied chord structure (they have recently been working on chords and the teacher has chosen the song partly because it makes a good link with this concept).
2. Listen to two different recorded performances of the spiritual and compare them.
3. Consider the meaning of the words and how the music expresses them (for example *a falling phrase which gives a feeling of weight and sadness*).
4. Ask students to hum through the roots and thirds of the chord pattern.
5. Hum a simple riff to go with the melody.
6. Analyse and discuss the phrase structure.
7. Take some of the musical material (for example *chords, phrases*) and explore them through composition.

8. Teach students some vocal technique (for example *effective breathing, avoidance of diphthongs*).
9. Relate the pentatonic nature of the music to other folk music from around the world.

The extra range of strategies employed means that learning is likely to be enhanced for a wider range of students. The tasks are also more challenging and have the potential to be musically interesting. The key question for the teacher to ask when planning this lesson(s) is: 'Which strategies will give me the outcome I want?'

Individual learning strategies
When considering the needs of individuals there are several factors that might be taken into account:

- direction and intervention in their learning can restrict some learners
- others may need to start with some kind of structure or framework
- some students can discover things for themselves
- others may be de-motivated by too much instruction.

Students need to be helped with their learning skills. For example do you *teach* students to:

- ask relevant questions of you and themselves (i.e. do not assume that they will be able to do this anyway)?
- experiment with sound and listen to expressive qualities (without placing undue emphasis on whether a note was right, wrong, in-tune, behind the beat)?
- change the order of sounds (for example *play them backwards, faster, slower*)?
- develop effective rehearsal technique (so that maximum benefit is obtained from practise and progress is maximized)?

Students need to feel motivated. Do you:

- celebrate what students can do?
- resist telling them what they can not do (directly or indirectly)?
- use a balance of praise and challenge?
- leave students feeling positive?
- have students arriving to lessons wanting to begin (because they can feel a sense of progress)?
- recognize progress (even with students whom you feel are behind)?
- recognize that some students, especially (but not exclusively) more capable learners, require a sense of challenge?

Differentiation for individuals

In a situation where the teacher knows students well, learning is likely to be more effective. Where a teacher is teaching many students for a short period of time each week he will not have the opportunity to know individuals as well. In some situations a more individual approach may be possible and the teacher could adapt his teaching to take account of individual needs. In examination groups for example:

Example 1

> *A Year 12 class with three students – Ian (grade 6 violin and grade 4 piano), Susan (grade 8 cello and grade 5 piano) and Sarah (grade 4 piano).*
>
> *The lesson starts with the students sitting an extract from the aural section of a past paper. Susan finds it very easy and learns little from the exercise. Ian struggles with the task and Sarah feels a sense of frustration. She begins to wonder if she should have taken this course.*
>
> *The group moves on to a study of set works. They listen to a recording of a Haydn Symphony and follow the score. The teacher dictates some notes to them (based on a published analysis and sets them an essay (based on a previous examination paper).*

In this lesson the teacher knows the students well. He has introduced activities that are closely related to the examination board syllabus. However, the lesson has missed opportunities to respond to the students' needs:

- Ian would benefit from more work on essay style and technique, research methods and organization of materials
- Sarah needs to develop aural skills through a range of singing and improvisation activities. She could also use a computer program to help. Tackling past papers merely reinforces her sense of failure
- Susan is an accomplished performer and has strong aural skills. She needs relatively little practise in this area. However her composition and improvisation skills are quite weak and are not being developed sufficiently. It would be helpful for her to consider for herself those areas of her musicianship requiring further improvement (even if not directly required by the examination syllabus).

The teaching of the set work does not encourage any of the students to respond to the music with sufficient insight or understanding. See chapter 9 for further information on post-16 teaching.

Example 2

> A Year 11 GCSE class. The class contains students with a variety of prior
> experiences – a grade 5 pianist, five students who have taken other graded
> examinations on instruments, five self-taught keyboard players and two rock
> guitarists. The teacher has based lessons on the GCSE syllabus and addresses
> the composition aspect by asking students to compose a melody. They will add
> an accompaniment at a later date. They are asked to compose a 12 or 16-bar
> melody using a computer, keyboard and sequencing software. After four lessons
> two students have managed this. The rest have made little progress.

In this lesson the teacher has tried to use ICT in order to enhance students'
work. The teacher is aware of students' prior experience but has not catered
sufficiently well for their needs.

The students are encouraged to focus on what their melody looks like
in musical notation (but very little emphasis is given to what it sounds
like). As a consequence the melodies consist of quavers, crotchets and
minims. They sound quite dull. Several students are capable of composing
complex and interesting melody patterns in a style which will not 'look
right' on the computer screen. They quickly lose interest in the task they
have been given. The teacher makes little evaluation of how effective ICT
has been in enhancing the students' outcomes and is pleased that they
have all had the opportunity to use the computer.

Example 3

> A visiting brass teacher has a group of three Year 8 students. James has played
> the trumpet for three years (for two of these a relative gave him lessons), but is
> not secure in reading music. Sally has been learning with the same teacher for
> two years and has passed grade 3. Jenny plays in a local brass training band.
> She has only been learning for two years but has made very good progress.
> Each student plays through the same scales and arpeggios (from Sally's
> examination syllabus). They then each play individual pieces (the other
> students sit and listen while they wait for their turn).

The teacher knows the students well. Although each has had some
individual attention they have spent nearly two thirds of the lesson
doing very little. The teacher might be able to devise some activities that
involve everyone. This could be some kind of ensemble playing (with
each student working at their own level) or through involving the
students in appraisal of each other's work and the application of key
points to their own performances.

Classroom management of students

One strategy used to help differentiation can be the ways in which students are grouped for teaching purposes. For example:

Small group work

This can be useful for developing social skills, speaking and listening and encouraging ensemble performance skills. It can also allow the teacher to:

■ target specific resources or instruments and individuals or groups
■ provide support for certain students (perhaps with the help of a Learning Support Assistant)
■ provide challenge for more experienced instrumentalists
■ encourage independence in learning.

Groups can be organized in four main ways:

1. Mixed ability

This will make organization and differentiation difficult. It will probably be most successful when setting an open-ended composition task where differentiation is achieved by outcome only.

2. Ability or prior experience groups

This grouping is most effective for differentiation by task. 'Ability' will need careful handling. For example the experienced instrumentalist might be less able in some contexts (requiring improvisation). Groups can be adjusted as work progresses. Even groups chosen in this way may contain a wide range of experience and interests.

3. Friendship groups

One or two students may dominate these groups. They may always adopt the same role or insist on using certain instruments. The group will need to be monitored carefully and may be difficult to manage (since friendship groups can change quite quickly, especially in Years 7 and 8).

4. Gender groups

This type of grouping is quite rare and does not appear to offer any obvious advantages.

Learning resources

When preparing resources, presentation can be helpful:

■ use short sentences and avoid unnecessary punctuation
■ keep language simple and direct
■ break up text into short paragraphs
■ restrict sentences to a maximum of ten words

■ do not put too much text on a page (leave spaces and use pictures or diagrams)
■ use printed fonts that are clear and easy to read
■ emphasize words or important points by using indentation, centre alignment, bold type or bullet points.

Resources for the less able

All the above points hold true for students who have less secure literacy skills. Additionally:

■ use worksheets sparingly
■ use familiar language
■ devise a vocabulary list for each new topic
■ use techniques such as multiple choice answers or cloze procedure (completing sentences with appropriate words) in order to allow success for students who find writing difficult
■ break learning down into small, manageable steps
■ give regular and positive feedback.

■ Some qualities of differentiated and undifferentiated teaching

Differentiation is a complex task and a few teachers will seem to manage it with little effort. Most of us will have to work hard in order to achieve success.

The following statements are intended as a checklist that might be used for a self-review process. The list is not definitive and you will almost certainly be able to add extra statements. Going through this with another teacher (even from another subject area) may provoke some useful discussion.

Some characteristics of differentiated teaching	Put a statement such as always, sometimes, never
Note is taken of information from feeder schools about prior attainment (N.B. not just a list of those who receive instrumental tuition).	
Lesson activities allow students to demonstrate a range of attainment.	
The teacher regularly celebrates success (in a range of musical styles and cultures).	

An assumption is not made that all music needs to be notated using stave notation.	
Clear information is given about the lesson's learning objective and that there is probably more than one way to achieve this.	
Students use resources which are appropriate to their needs (for example *they are not asked to compose complex pieces using just tuned percussion*).	
Students develop skills during Key Stage 3 which are sufficient to enable any of them to take GCSE music.	
The teacher works with groups and individuals in a targeted way (which takes account of their prior experience and their interests).	
The teacher and the student discuss the ways in which the student learns most effectively.	
Some tasks are sufficiently open-ended to allow all students the opportunity to make sufficient progress.	
Marking and verbal comments give students sufficient information for them to understand how to improve.	
The teacher does not assume that all students are at the same point in their learning.	
The pace of a lesson is not always dictated by the whole class.	
Students are not over-directed by the teacher.	
Students are given targets to help them to improve their learning.	
Different musical styles and cultures are given equal value.	

Skills are taught on a regular basis (so that students feel a sense of progress).	
The quality of a musical outcome is as important as its complexity (for example *students sing unison songs expressively, with good tone quality and control of dynamics – rather than three part pieces which lack control and tone quality*).	

Summary points:

■ Meeting individual needs is complex. It requires an insight into how students learn, what is success, how to respond to a diversity of interests and how to plan effectively.

■ Medium-term planning (for example *a scheme of work*) will probably assume about three levels of outcome (for example *working towards expectation, at expectation and working above expectation*) but a more individualized approach is desirable.

■ Short-term planning (for example *lesson planning*) will respond much more to individual needs and will change from year to year.

5

Teaching and learning

Aim: this chapter sets out some information about what makes teaching effective. This is related to relevant information such as inspections, performance management and national initiatives such as literacy and numeracy.

◼ Effective teaching and learning

It is generally accepted that good teachers make a big difference to the quality of a student's educational experience. In this country we are fortunate to have many inspiring teachers. Some work exclusively in schools or FE, others work in higher education or LEAs. Collectively they have exerted a strong influence on the musical education of students.

Teaching is a complex area and there are several factors which will affect learning:

1. Students will probably not make good progress if they are not motivated or interested. A good teacher may inspire them to become motivated. However although a teacher may have success with one group of students in one type of school it does not follow that the same teacher will be equally successful in another school. Different circumstances may require new techniques and skills.
2. Teachers need to be effective in order to ensure that good progress is made. Definitions of what is meant by the term 'effective' will vary. What works for one teacher may not work for another. For example *a teacher who embraces the latest technology, is very energetic and appears to be effective to the casual observer may not actually be as effective as someone who appears to be very quiet and is suspicious of new ideas.* The best indicator of effective teaching is always likely to be how well students are learning.
3. Sometimes progress is very obvious, on other occasions it is more complex and difficult to detect. There may appear to be quick progress in one particular lesson but insufficient progress over time. Conversely there may be good progress over time but a particular lesson does not

work well or has shortcomings. Some students may be making good progress whereas others, for example *students with special educational needs,* make insufficient progress. Post-16 students may make more rapid progress towards the end of their course as ideas, skills and information are drawn together and consolidated. Progress needs to be considered in the short-term (for example *a lesson*), medium-term (for example *a school term*) and the long-term (for example *a year or Key Stage*). Progress across a lesson or half-term may not mean secure progress in the long-term. For example *students in Year 8 make good progress when completing a composition project. By the time they are ready to make their option choices in Year 9 very few have secure performance skills and consequently feel that GCSE music is not a realistic option for them.* The progress of these students over time is less secure.

4. Progress means better quality as well as more complexity. Students should be encouraged to use expressive control in their compositions and performances whenever possible. For example *use of tone quality, dynamics and phrasing.* They should be encouraged to respond to these elements in music they listen to and appraise. This will help to encourage a classroom where quality is valued and emphasized.

5. Progress applies to students' attitudes as well as to their skills and knowledge. For example *students who know information because they have been rigorously taught and tested, but do not value music may have missed out on an important aspect of their musical development.* Students who receive instrumental lessons and who can only perform in one style or genre will probably have missed a key aspect of their development.

Progress in learning

Progress in music education can occur through:

1. Depth and development of knowledge. For example *students know more factual information about music, they know the names of more pieces of music and composers, they know an increasing number of technical words and can apply them in the right context.* Although important too much of this activity or insufficient links with what music sounds like can give rise to activities which are unmusical.

2. Development of understanding. This is very important and one of the most challenging tasks for any teacher. For example *students are increasingly able to make their own judgements about music, they make their own decisions about compositions and performances, they apply their understanding of musical concepts to their own compositions and they are able to recognize key aspects of music in pieces they listen to for the first time.*

3. Development of skills. Over a period of time students need to develop important skills. For example *they are able to perform more fluently and with more expression in Year 9 than in Year 8, they write and talk about music with increasing sophistication.*

4. Development of attitudes. For example *over a period of time students begin to listen to a wider range of music, they develop an open outlook and are prepared to try new ideas, they become adaptable and enquiring.*

5. A broadening of experience. As students move through a Key Stage they may be introduced to new experiences or opportunities. This broadening can lead to progression. For example *students encounter a wide range of musical styles and are encouraged to play by ear and from notation.* Occasionally it can lead to a lack of progression. For example *in Year 9 students are all asked to play the guitar (having previously played mainly keyboards). Most find this difficult and they are not able to play fluently or with any expression. This demotivates and de-skills them just at the time when they are considering their option choices.*

6. The increasing quality of the outcome. This is one of the most important elements of progression. For example *as students move through Key Stage 3 they are expected to sing with increasing expression. In Year 9 they sing songs which are technically simple, but to a good standard. This enables the boys with changing voices to still participate in this activity (and feel a sense of achievement and quality).*

Effective teaching

As we have noted, progress in learning requires effective teaching. What are the factors which make teaching effective?

A few contextual factors need to be considered:

1. Anything that involves interactions between human beings will contain many variable factors. Teaching is no exception. There are no simple answers. Every class and every teacher is unique. There is no easily applied formula which will work equally well with them all.

2. Teachers appear to be the one factor which makes the biggest difference. Therefore a detailed description of a lesson plan will probably be interesting and valuable. However the same lesson may be more, or less, effective when delivered by another teacher in a different context. For example *because of a particular emphasis given to something, reference to previous activities or because a particular teacher is a very effective communicator.* Often these subtle differences which make all the difference are difficult to identify or to write down.

3. Nearly all of us can improve our teaching. One way to do this is to consider the work of others. Having done so we may want to use ideas

in our work, adapt them to suit our circumstances or reject them because they do not seem relevant. See chapter 11 for more information on self-review.

4. There are other factors which can affect teaching and learning. Accommodation can make a big difference to the success of a lesson. For example *in an environment where there is a great deal of noise students may struggle to make progress or to produce work of quality, perhaps using dynamic contrast or phrasing.* Resources can make a similar difference. For example *where students are sharing two or three to a keyboard they may struggle to make progress and may not produce work of quality.* However, on their own, improved resources or accommodation may not result in improved teaching.

5. The amount of time students spend on an activity is important and will have an effect on progress. For example *if students spend less than 70 minutes a week in music lessons they may be receiving insufficient time to cover fully the National Curriculum Programmes of Study. An assumption was made when planning the National Curriculum that students would spend about 45 hours per year in music lessons during Key Stage 3. Where students have a block of music for one term and then a large gap before returning to it they are likely to forget information and may find it difficult to maintain skill levels.*

One source, which tries to describe characteristics of effective teaching, is the Threshold Assessment Documentation (DFEE 1999). Good teachers are required to demonstrate some key characteristics, as detailed below:

Professional knowledge and understanding

- have a sound and up-to-date knowledge of good practice in teaching techniques relevant to the subject(s) or specialism(s) and students taught
- know their subject(s) or specialism(s) in sufficient depth and teach effectively
- take account of curriculum developments outside their immediate area of interest which are relevant to their own work
- be aware of national strategies that are relevant to them, for example *literacy, numeracy*, information and communications technology, and have incorporated them as appropriate into their teaching.

Teaching and assessment

- plan lessons and sequences of lessons to meet students' individual learning needs

- use a range of appropriate strategies for teaching and classroom management
- use information about prior attainment to set well-grounded expectations for students and monitor progress to give clear and constructive feedback.

Student progress

- students achieve well relative to the students' prior attainment, making progress as good or better than similar students nationally. This should be shown in marks or grades in any relevant national tests or examinations, or school based assessment for students where national tests and examinations are taken.

Wider professional effectiveness

- take responsibility for their professional development and use the outcomes to improve their teaching and students' learning
- make an active contribution to the policies and aspirations of the school.

Professional characteristics

- are effective professionals who challenge and support all students to do their best.

Similarly the most recent OFSTED inspection handbook (1999: 44) defines those aspects of teaching and learning which HMI consider to be important. The OFSTED handbook gives some exemplification materials but very few which relate directly to music teaching. The OFSTED criteria are listed below and an example of what this might mean in music lessons has been added.

In determining their judgements, inspectors should consider the extent to which teachers:	*In an effective lesson this might be shown by:*
Show good subject knowledge and understanding in the way they present and discuss their subject.	For Key Stage 3 lessons, subject knowledge is usually more than sufficient (since the great majority of teachers are music 'specialists'). When teaching older students, the subject knowledge requirements are likely to be much more demanding. For example *in a Year 13 A level lesson the*

	teacher is able to demonstrate sections of some Haydn, Mozart and Beethoven piano sonatas with great fluency. As he does so he challenges the students to consider how each composer develops the sonata form structure of some movements and how the composers influenced each other.
Are technically competent in teaching basic skills.	Basic skills refer to spelling, punctuation, adding, subtracting and so on. However we could apply the term to musical basic skills such as singing or performing on an instrument. For example *in a Year 11 GCSE lesson the teacher works with the students on some unaccompanied singing. Although not a trained singer she has a sound understanding of how to sing effectively and can communicate this in a way which the students find easy to understand. She has done this regularly since the start of Year 10 and the students have developed their singing skills and confidence, as well as improving their aural skills.*
Plan effectively, setting clear objectives that students understand.	Planning includes short, medium and long-term planning. For example *a teacher is working with a Year 8 class. The long and medium-term planning is set out clearly in departmental documentation (which shows a clear progression from Year 7 to Year 13). The teacher bases his short-term planning on this scheme. In this Year 8 class of 28 students there are three on the special educational needs register and five who have instrumental lessons. The lesson plan takes account of the needs of these students, draws on work they have all done in Year 7 and includes effective 'I can do' self-assessment sheets for the students to complete.*
Challenge and inspire students, expecting the most of them, so as to deepen their knowledge and understanding.	This requires the teacher to ensure that students are not overwhelmed or lost during the lesson, whilst expecting very high standards. For example *in a Year 12 performing arts course students are studying 'conflict' and look at this through music. They consider ways to set aspects of the mass (representing resolution) and look at war*

	poetry, especially from World War I. Late in the term they look at the music from Britten's 'War Requiem'. They find the emotional context of this piece to be very powerful. They attend a performance. For several students this will be their first encounter with a 'classical music' concert. None have heard any music by Britten before. Three listen to Britten's 'Missa Brevis' as further individual research.
Use methods which enable all students to learn effectively.	There are a variety of methods. They could include use of questioning, purpose of practical activities, student groupings. They will suit the needs of the students being taught. For example *some Year 7 students have been composing pieces based on the idea of a 'rondo'. Towards the end of the lesson the teacher chooses three groups to play their pieces (there is not time for all the groups to be heard). The groups have been chosen to exemplify particular points. After each group has performed, the teacher asks members of the group and the rest of the class a series of questions. These allow all students to understand further some of the key points about a rondo and each group is asked to set one target for completion of the project in the next lesson.*
Manage students well and insist on high standards of behaviour.	In some schools management will rarely be a problem. In others it may be more of a challenge. For example *in a Year 9 lesson students are looking at chord progressions. There are several students who lack motivation. The teacher manages this by maintaining a positive and supportive relationship with these students and gives appropriate extra support to two students who are finding the work difficult. She does this by breaking down the activity into short-term, achievable targets. She also chooses some repertoire that is in the current charts and the students respond positively to this.*
Use time, support staff and other resources, especially information and communications technology, effectively.	The use of time is very important. The use of information and communications technology needs to have a clear musical purpose. For example *in a Year 12 BTEC*

	popular music lesson students each use a computer, sequencer and a keyboard to develop their compositions. They load work saved from the previous lesson and work on their own using headphones. They use the software with skill and are able to try new ideas, add new parts and change the timbre of the sounds as required. The technology is used well to enhance their performance skills.
Assess students' work thoroughly and use assessments to help and encourage students to overcome difficulties.	The type of assessment referred to in the OFSTED framework is what might be termed day-to-day. It would include marking, questioning and plenary sessions. For example *during a Year 8 lesson the teacher moves around to monitor the progress of different groups. He notices that several students are not using all five fingers of their right hand to play keyboards (some use alternate fingers from different hands and very few make use of their thumb). At the start of the next lesson the teacher gets the class to practise this technique. The students then carry on with their project, this time having greater success due to their improved fluency.*
Use homework effectively to reinforce and/or extend what is learned in school.	Homework may be relevant for Key Stage 3 students. It will be an integral part of examination courses. For example *Year 13 students are studying Stravinsky's 'Rite of Spring'. The teacher has put information about the piece (background notes, past paper questions and a schedule of homework tasks) on to the school's website. Students access this during their free periods, lessons and from home.*

And the extent to which students:	*In an effective lesson, or sequence of lessons this might be shown by:*
Acquire new knowledge or skill, develop ideas and increase their understanding.	Students develop their knowledge, skills and understanding during lessons, across the medium-term (for example *a term*) and across a Key Stage. For example *a group of Year 9 students have been working on the use of modes in their compositions. They have*

	done this securely and nearly all can name two modes, play the mode on an instrument and have used them within a composition. Later in the project they listen to some recorded music and most students are able to recognize that examples drawn from different periods, styles and cultures make similar use of modes.
Apply intellectual, physical or creative effort in their work.	Music lessons may require considerable intellectual and creative effort. For example *a group of Year 13 students have been composing pieces based on one of their set works (Stravinsky's 'Soldier's Tale'). They have researched the piece on the Internet, a CD-ROM and using textbooks. Having decided on some of the key features of the piece they have then composed ideas based on dance rhythms, chorales and irregular time signatures.*
Are productive and work at a good pace.	In most lessons the pace of students' work will be affected by how well they understand the task, the degree of challenge set by the teacher and the expectation that work will be completed within a designated time frame. For example *in a Year 10 lesson students are used to being given a target time for completing tasks. They realize that the teacher will expect them to have completed a task during this time and that they will probably be expected to perform their work to the rest of the group. This helps them to work at a good pace.*
Show interest in their work, are able to sustain concentration and think for themselves.	Students should be encouraged to increasingly apply their understanding of music to new situations. For example *students in a choir are encouraged to make their own decisions about tempi, phrasing and dynamics. They are taught vocal technique, which they apply to new pieces. When technical problems arise they are encouraged to analyse why and choose appropriate strategies for improvement.*
Understand what they are doing, how well they have done and how they can improve.	Effective teaching will allow students to understand the progress they are making and set themselves targets for

improvement. For example *Year 8 students are working on a blues project. They have been given information about what might be expected by the end of the project and the teacher uses effective questioning to ensure that the students have a clear idea of what they have done, what to do next and how to improve their work.*

Factors which might make teaching less effective

There are several factors that can lead to teaching being less effective. Some of these may be caused by particular individual circumstances, such as accommodation or resources. There are other factors:

1. The teacher lacks subject knowledge. For example *is not familiar with popular musical styles and is therefore unable to use these within lessons. The teacher is also negative about this style of music and projects this attitude to the students.*
2. Notation is taught in isolation from other musical skills. For example *students make up words such as 'CABBAGE' and notate them onto manuscript paper. Writing the music out occupies the students for a considerable period of time.*
3. Students are given activities to complete but are not clear about the purpose, what level to aim at or how they can improve.
4. Some musical skills are valued more highly than others. For example *performing pieces from written notation rather than improvisation.*
5. Activities are not integrated well. For example *GCSE students have one lesson on composition and one lesson on listening. They do not make links between these activities.*
6. Students are not taught how to solve technical problems. For example *students use keyboards but by the end of Year 9 are still not able to use their thumb, all five fingers or cross their thumb under when performing.*
7. Planning does not take account of long-term progression. For example *teachers plan individual lessons and projects effectively but do not consider how these projects inter-link, or give sufficient attention to planning across a complete Key Stage.*
8. Little information is collected on prior learning. For example *an assumption is made that Year 6 students know very little. The music*

department's liaison programme consists of the school band going to perform at the local primary school. No information is collected on the Key Stage 2 curriculum and the secondary music teacher believes, wrongly, that the primary teacher will not be effective because she is not a specialist. Although the primary teacher lacks confidence (particularly when talking to the secondary specialist) she is a very effective teacher.

Organization of teaching groups

In Key Stage 3 teaching activity often consists of students working in groups. This is often the result of necessity, rather than a philosophical decision that group-work is the most appropriate method of classroom organization. Of course there are advantages to be gained from successful group activities. Students will need to develop:

- negotiation skills
- effective listening skills
- ways of working which are flexible. For example *taking it in turns to lead.*

There are potential disadvantages to this way of working as well. These need to be borne in mind:

- insufficient resources may mean some students playing untuned percussion instruments because they are the only instruments left, rather than because it will develop their skills or understanding. This may lead to a lack of progress. Wherever possible all students should be given access to a range of resources. These should include the best quality sound resources possible, including instruments, which can sustain sounds effectively (not just percussion instruments)
- sharing musical space is sometimes difficult. For example *two students work together on a keyboard, using headphones. Although working 'together' they are actually trying to work on their own for this project. A similar scenario might be if they were trying to paint a picture by sharing the same paints, brushes and canvas.* Where possible students should have the opportunity to work individually, in pairs and in groups. The tasks given should match these groupings. For example *if students are developing individual skills they may need to work individually*
- some students will tend to dominate groups and others may have little opportunity to put forward ideas or develop sufficiently. The teacher will need to be aware of this and manage the groups accordingly. For example *getting students to take it in turns to lead*

■ friendship groups are very volatile, particularly with younger students. Considerable time can be wasted as students adjust and re-adjust to whom they like to work with. It may be helpful to limit the use of friendship groupings.

Timing and pace

The amount of time given to particular activities is very important and can have a big effect on learning. In chapter 2 we considered some of the short-term planning of a teacher working on a blues project. In lesson 6 of the project the lesson was described in this way:

Lesson 6	1. The groups are reminded of their target and begin work. Some adjust their chord sequence from a standard 12-bar blues to a later style. They research this information using a CD-ROM and the Internet. All groups perform at the end of the lesson and are set a target for the next lesson. 2. The class sings a blues song and focuses on stylistic devices, such as bending the pitch of certain notes in order to add a blues 'feel' to the piece.

The lesson is 60 minutes long. A more detailed breakdown of what might have happened in this lesson follows here:

Time	Description of activity
9.00	The class arrives. The teacher reminds the class that each group and some individuals were given a target for this lesson. They are asked to consider what these were. They take their instruments and start work.
9.05	The teacher moves around the groups. They have been organized according to their prior experience and attainment. A classroom assistant supports one group, with a statemented student. The groups move quickly into the task, refining and improving their work. The teacher works with a group who are adapting the standard twelve bar blues to C7/F7/C7/C7/F7/F7/C7/C7/D-7/G7/C7/G7// (they have found this out by research on a CD-ROM and the Internet).
9.30	The students quickly re-assemble and play through their pieces. The teacher asks some effective questions, which help the students' understanding. For example *what was effective about this performance,*

	if this group have trouble performing the piece at this tempo what could they do to help them to practise it more effectively, which chord are we on now (having asked a group to stop at a certain point), does it sound better with the seventh or without, what would happen if they played the piece faster?
9.45	Instruments and equipment are put away.
9.50	The class sing through 'In the mood'. They add vocal riffs as an accompaniment. They work on a middle, improvised section and practise some phrases which require them to sing 'blue' notes.
9.58	They listen to a recording where the singer is singing a blues piece effectively by giving emphasis to 'blue' notes. They discuss the tempo of the piece and how important it is when improvising to leave silent 'gaps' in phrases.
10.00	The teacher congratulates the class on their work. She reminds them that they will be evaluating their progress next lesson using the cards they were given at the start of the project.

Another teacher covering the same projects and with very similar aims and methods manages the lesson in this way:

Time	Description of activity
9.00	The class arrives. The teacher reminds the class that each group and some individuals were given a target for this lesson. They are asked to consider what these were. The teacher goes around the class and asks each group what their targets are. They take their instruments and start work.
9.15	The teacher moves around the groups (organized according to friendship). Two students do not want to work together. The teacher spends ten minutes sorting out the groups and reorganizing two of them in order to accommodate the hurt feelings of one of the students. A classroom assistant supports one group, with a statemented student. The groups work on their pieces but the disruption has meant that three groups do not make much progress at the start of this session. The teacher works with a group who are adapting the standard 12-bar blues to C7/F7/C7/C7/F7/F7/C7/C7/D-7/G7/C7/G7// (they have found this out by research on a CD-ROM and the Internet).

9.35	The teacher had planned to ask the students to perform their piece at this point but decides they need more time. The pace of students' work begins to slow.
9.50	The students re-assemble. The teacher decides that there will not be time for all groups to perform their pieces. He asks two groups to play. He makes general, positive comments to each group. Although supportive the comments are not specific enough and do not help the students to understand how to improve their work. The other students listen but are not actively involved.
9.58	Instruments and equipment are put away.
10.00	The teacher congratulates the class on their work. He comments that they have not had time to sing the song today but hopes that they may be able to do so next week.

Although the planning of these lessons is very similar the outcomes are different. Both lessons are effective but the first example is particularly good and the students make more progress. In the first lesson the things that helped to make the lesson effective were:

■ the timing of the lesson (students realize that they are all likely to be required to perform at the end of the lesson and that if the teacher says this will be at 9.30 then this is their target)
■ effective use of questioning to draw out understanding
■ a clear focus on what the teacher wants to achieve.

Over a period of time the differences in these lessons, if replicated, may add up to a significant difference in students' experiences and progress.

Literacy and Numeracy Strategies

Government strategies have been introduced into Key Stages 1 and 2. The aim has been to improve attainment, particularly for 11-year-old students. It is planned that these strategies will continue into Key Stage 3. A key part of these strategies has been to give teachers detailed schemes and lesson plans. Another aspect has been the inclusion of information on how a model lesson should be taught. This gives a quite detailed description of what current views on 'effective teaching' look like. What is recommended and can it be applied to music lessons?

In the National Numeracy Strategy, the following general points are made:

■ in each lesson the teacher should spend as much time as possible in direct teaching and questioning of the whole class, a group of students, or individuals

■ high quality direct teaching is oral, interactive and lively (not lecturing or expecting students to teach themselves)

■ it is a two-way process and students should play an active part by answering questions, contributing points to discussions and explaining their methods to the class.

The key point being made here is about what constitutes 'direct teaching'. The description could give an impression of the teacher in the sole role as 'director' This might require relatively little input from students. There is, however, rather more to this notion of direct teaching than initially meets the eye.

If we were to apply this model to music teaching we might decide that good direct teaching is achieved by balancing different elements:

■ **directing:** sharing teaching objectives with the class, ensuring that students know what to do, and drawing attention to points over which they should take particular care. For example *asking students to reflect on what they have to do before they start a practical activity*

■ **instructing:** giving information and structuring it well. For example *ensuring that students know how to solve a technical problem such as the use of the thumb when playing a keyboard*

■ **demonstrating:** showing an idea. For example *demonstrating how the blues scale can fit over a 12-bar blues*

■ **explaining and illustrating:** giving accurate explanations and referring to previous work when appropriate. For example *pointing out that students have already dealt with chords in Year 7 before moving on to the addition of sevenths in Year 8*

■ questioning and discussing: questioning in ways which match the direction and pace of the lesson and ensure that over a period of time all students take part, listening carefully to students' responses and using open and closed questions.

Summary points:

Teaching is a complex activity. There is no simple formula which can be applied to all classes or schools. Each teacher and group of students is different. However, teachers make the biggest difference to how well students learn. There are a number of factors that can contribute to this:

■ subject knowledge, teaching skills and pedagogy
■ resources and accommodation
■ the management of students and the maintenance of a positive relationship
■ short, medium and long-term planning
■ effective use of assessment
■ integration of activities
■ lessons with pace and good organization.

6

Integrating ICT into the music curriculum

Aim: this chapter looks at how Information and Communications Technology is changing our lives and the implications this has for music teaching.

The impact of new technology

New technologies are causing a major industrial, economic and social revolution. This is having an effect on many aspects of our lives. The pace of change is rapid and it is very difficult to come to an accurate assessment of how much further change is likely. We are probably in the midst of a change as profound as the industrial revolution of the 19th century, or that brought about by the introduction of printing. We are entering an 'information age' where citizens of the future will require very different skills to those required in the current 'industrial age'. History tells us that this type of change makes a strong impact on social structures and the fabric of society. Education is a key part of this structure and music teaching is likely to be affected. Learning will change and students will be able to gain access to information from numerous sources. A school may not be the main focus for learning. The last decade has seen falling costs (in real terms), greater computer processing power and matched increases in the sophistication of software (often leading to enhanced interface with the user). It has also seen an increase in the pace of new changes and initiatives. Today's children will be entering a different world to the one that exists today and will require a range of new skills.

The future will probably offer challenges and opportunities. At present we can only glimpse some of these. Likely changes that we can see, at the moment, include:

- further increases in computer power (this is currently doubling every eighteen months) coupled with machines which are increasingly smaller and more portable
- increases in memory storage capacity and use of 'smart cards'

- ■ flat screen monitors
- ■ smaller, lighter computers as common as calculators are today
- ■ increased use of mobile phones (used more and more for Internet access)
- ■ interactive software that increasingly recognizes gesture and voice commands
- ■ new kinds of knowledge, new ways of handling information (for example *real audio, MP3*) and downloading of digital information from the Internet
- ■ increase of 'e-commerce' (business conducted using the Internet)
- ■ convergence of telephones, computers and television (as a result of digital technology). These will give increased access to interactive services, shopping, banking and distance learning
- ■ a more sophisticated 'learning environment', capable of replacing several of the core functions of teachers. This may leave teachers to play a more creative role and remove some of their responsibility for more mundane tasks. For example *mediating and managing learning at home, in school and in resource centres (such as libraries) as education extends beyond school boundaries*
- ■ students working from home for part of the week (perhaps coming together for sport, music and social activities)
- ■ technology affecting most traditional instrument manufacture, recording and performance venues. It will probably change the way instruments are taught.

We can see a glimpse of this type of change starting to happen in a number of today's schools. New technology has made a very strong impact on contemporary popular music, and this can be heard on radio and television. New sounds and ways of accessing them are increasingly available in shops and on the Internet.

The implications of change

The implications of all these potential changes are difficult to assess. Some may have unexpected effects and others will be quickly overtaken by even newer developments which we, as yet, are unaware of. All professional educators will need to feel competent and confident in the use of new technologies. In the music department of the next ten years technology will affect organization, management and teaching:

1. There will be a need for schools to develop a code of ethics about the use of new technologies (such as scanners). An important part of this will include copyright in recorded and published music. Students and teachers will need to work within a Code of Practice. Students will

probably need to explore some of these points in order to come to their own understanding of intellectual property, plagiarism and appropriate acknowledgement.

2. Teachers and students will need to develop strategies for searching for information (in order to access appropriate materials efficiently). This is an area that will develop further as commerce becomes interested in building up profiles of personal use and preferences. There are ethical points about these profiles and the place in society of those without access to technology, which may need to be covered with students.
3. Schools and music departments will be developing increasingly sophisticated websites. Information will be available 24 hours a day and traditional activities (such as handwriting or writing notation) may become less common.
4. Greater use might be made of technology to present materials in classrooms. For example *data projectors, electronic white-boards*.

The National Curriculum Orders

The most recent National Curriculum Orders have strengthened further the place of ICT within all subjects.

In the National Curriculum Orders for music (QCA 1999) reference is made to the expected use of ICT within each Key Stage:

During the Key Stage, pupils should be taught the knowledge, skills and understanding through:

- *Using ICT to capture, change and combine sounds*
  Breadth of Study Key Stage 2 5b (p. 19)

- *Using ICT to create, manipulate and refine sounds*
  Breadth of Study Key Stage 3 5d (p. 21)

Additionally, each National Curriculum Order contains information about the use of information and communication technology across the curriculum:

Pupils should be given opportunities to apply and develop their ICT capability through the use of ICT tools to support their learning in all subjects (with the exception of physical education at Key Stages 1 and 2).

Pupils should be given opportunities to support their work by being taught to:
a. find things out from a variety of sources, selecting and synthesizing the information to meet their needs and developing an ability to question its accuracy, bias and plausibility

b. develop their ideas using ICT tools to amend and refine their work and enhance its quality and accuracy
c. exchange and share information, both directly and through electronic media
d. review, modify and evaluate their work, reflecting critically on its quality, as it progresses.

(p. 34)

Implicit reference to the use of ICT is also included in the National Curriculum's 'General teaching requirements'. For example:

Using ICT for pupils with special educational needs in order to:
■ help with communication, language and literacy
■ increase pupils' knowledge of the wider world.

Using ICT to support pupils who are learning English as an additional language by:
■ providing support using ICT, video or audio materials.

Some pupils may require:
■ access to adapted instruments or ICT to overcome difficulties with mobility or manipulative skills.

Examination courses

Music examination courses make increasing use of new technology. Examination boards now commonly accept computer files as examples of coursework or sequenced compositions. There has also been a growth in students taking music technology examination courses and it is possible that these courses may have attracted a wider range of students than previously took a traditional A level course. Access to new technology may make music in schools more attractive to students than traditional music making on its own.

The contribution of ICT to music education

There are two aspects to the contribution that ICT might make to music education. The first, and probably most important, is the way that new technology (in various forms) can enable students to attain better results, gain access to quality experiences and have their work enhanced. The second is the contribution to ICT skills, what is often termed 'capability'. It is possible that effective use of ICT in music will make a contribution to students' general abilities to use these resources confidently and appropriately.

The contribution of ICT to attainment in music

The 1998 Music Technology in Action guide (BECTA) suggests ways that ICT can contribute to music education:

	Use and investigate sounds and structures	Refine and enhance performances and compositions	Extend awareness and knowledge of musical styles
Recording equipment	Explore ways to re-use sounds in new contexts. Explore musical textures using multi-track recorders. Explore structures by editing tapes or wave files.	Refine work after they have listened to it. Perform with a pre-recorded accompaniment. Capture a definitive performance to present to others.	Appraise what they have composed or performed. Listen to and discuss the music of others. Develop aural skills.
MIDI and sequencing equipment	Explore changes in tempo, register and instrumentation in their own work and that of others. Explore and make creative choices concerning musical structures and textures.	Perform and compose music using suitable switches and sensors that allow for limited movement or control. Add to and refine compositions using simple recording and editing procedures. Allow compositional ideas to advance beyond the constraints of limited motor skills or technique.	Explore off-the-shelf MIDI file arrangements to identify stylistic characteristics. Apply increasing skills of aural discrimination and awareness to decision-making and editing.
Keyboards	Explore and create harmonic polyphonic textures.	Perform music on their own and in ensembles.	Analyses the musical character of different auto-accompaniment styles.

	Explore and create music using different accompaniment styles. Try out different sounds and tempos and select from alternatives.	Enhance their work selectively using auto-accompaniment features.	Develop their understanding of the characteristics of musical sound.
CD-ROM	Explore and make creative choices concerning musical structures and textures. Explore the musical elements through structured learning programmes.	Learn more about how to play a particular piece or instrument. Create detailed compositions using detailed CD-ROM-based sequencing applications.	Listen to and discuss professional performances. Find out more about the music they study and about musical theory. Learn about music and instruments from different times and places.
Synthesizers and sound processors	Design, create and use new sounds. Explore how various controls can modify sound to achieve a desired effect.	Enhance and characterize performances and compositions by using appropriate sounds, reverberation or other effects.	Develop their understanding of the characteristics of musical sound. Learn which effects are appropriate to which musical styles.
The Internet	Download sounds in the form of wave files that can be loaded into samplers and used in compositions and performances.	Develop collaborative composition projects with pupils anywhere in the world.	Search for information about instruments, music and musicians from experts, organizations and libraries. Exchange files containing their own performances, compositions, opinions and sound resources with others

			anywhere in the world.
Drill and practice software		Encourage better performing skills (e.g. through rhythm and memory exercises).	Reinforce knowledge and skills concerning staff notation, keyboard layout and aural recognition.

What is meant by the term ICT 'capability'?

The term refers to how well a student can use computers, software and other electronic equipment. A student's capability is determined by how well he or she can:

- analyse information
- process information
- present information
- model information
- measure and control external events.

For example:

- **Analyse information:** *search a CD-ROM to find out how a particular instrument sounds*
- **Process information:** *enter information on a database and answer questions such as 'Is the longest instrument the heaviest?'*
- **Present information:** *produce a presentation which combines pictures, text and compositions*
- **Model information:** *compose a musical phrase, copy it, change the timbre and alter the tempo of some phrases*
- **Measure and control external events:** *record sounds into a sampler and use them as part of a composition which is played back controlled by a computer.*

What equipment should I have?

Hardware

Hardware means the computer, or other equipment (such as sampler, drum machine or four-track recorder). Your requirements will be dictated by several factors:

- the equipment you already have

- what expertise you already have
- what you require the hardware to do
- your budget
- any whole-school ICT policy.

If you already have a computer it is worth doing some research into what it might be able to do. Alternatively there may be computers around school which are not used effectively (perhaps because they are old). They may be useful. Some computers have built-in sounds (with a sound card); others do not but may be capable of controlling external sounds played on a keyboard. Some have both facilities and most modern computers fall into this category. In order to control other sounds a computer needs a Musical Instrument Digital Interface (MIDI) port. These can usually be purchased cheaply and added to the computer.

Computers

A computer with a sound card may also include a CD-ROM player. The player acts like an extra computer drive but the compact disc (CD) is capable of holding about six hundred times more information than a conventional floppy disc. These 'multimedia' computers can combine sound, video, text and images. They are increasingly common. Some computers are also able to run DVD technology. This gives access to even greater amounts of information (which often results in an 'interactive' interface with the user).

The price of hardware such as computers is often in direct proportion to its capability and power. As software becomes more and more sophisticated there is a consequent requirement for more powerful computer memory space and processing speed. This means that when considering new purchases it is well worth thinking ahead. The computer that runs today's software may become outdated very quickly. The more powerful the computer you purchase the longer it is likely to last.

When purchasing a computer take advice and compare like with like. Cost is not necessarily a good indicator of value for money. A modern computer should have:

- a 586 processor or above
- CD/DVD drive
- a sound card with midi
- at least an 80 MB hard disk (the larger the better)
- Internet access either through a standard telephone line (analogue) or digital line.

It is important to remember to include software, which can be expensive, in your budget.

Keyboards

Keyboards have transformed music teaching in a relatively short space of time. They:

- provide students with a wide range of sound sources (usually over 100 sounds)
- have increasingly high quality sound reproduction
- are relatively cheap
- are useful for learning about harmony.

When purchasing a keyboard it is helpful to consider what you wish to use it for (rather than necessarily going for the one that seems to do most things for the price). For example:

- touch sensitivity will allow greater control over expression
- a MIDI port will mean that it has the flexibility to be connected to a computer
- weighted keys give more of a 'feel' (and greater expressive control)
- the range of the keyboard (usually the more notes available the better)
- in-built amplification (otherwise you will require a separate amplifier)
- whether the sound is sampled or synthesized. This will affect the tone quality. Digitally sampled sounds generally give superior quality than synthesized sounds but may be more expensive
- demonstration tunes are usually a disadvantage.

Other useful equipment

- tape recorders
- multi-track recorders
- mini disc recording equipment (for digital quality sound)
- CD writer (in order to transfer large amounts of sound onto an easily accessible format)
- mixers
- drum machines
- samplers
- MIDI guitars and wind instruments
- MIDI microphone.

The functions of all these items of equipment are becoming increasingly available using a high specification computer and appropriate software. The cost of this equipment varies widely but costs are continually falling. An electronic keyboard costing £100 may represent good value compared to a tuned percussion instrument costing over twice as much.

Software

Software means programs which can be run on a computer. Some software is suitable for any curriculum area, other types are specific to music. For example:

Sequencing

Sequencing means recording short musical ideas and then joining, repeating or transposing them. The software can allow the user to experiment with ideas in a creative way. For example *a student might work on a piece over several weeks, saving it each time onto the school network, or a floppy disc. The student may be able to complete some work for homework (e-mailing it from school to home so that it is ready for further development). The student is able to edit his or her piece so that it is continually improved and adjusted.*

Drill and practice software

Some software is set up in order to practise a particular skill. For example:

■ notation writing skills
■ aural training.

With careful use they can be effective. However, very few are creative and while they can be used as a way of occupying students, they offer limited musical experience and development.

Music publishing

Most sequencers have the facility to show and print out a score. One or two pieces of software are specifically dedicated to this task. They often do this very well and for some students and teachers can be useful for example, when a teacher uses the software to print out music for the school band or orchestra. They are rarely creative and assume detailed knowledge of staff notation and a Western, classical approach. Their weakness as a creative tool is that the student will be required to focus on what the music looks like rather than what it sounds like.

CD-ROM

CD-ROMs contain a lot of information in a multimedia format (combining text, pictures and sound). Some are general (such as an encyclopaedia) but may contain useful musical information. Others are specifically written for music. Relatively few are written for music education and the large majority are produced for a general adult entertainment market (often known as 'edutainment'). This means that careful selection of these resources will need to be made. CD-ROMs provide a similar type of resource to the Internet.

Internet

The Internet is a burgeoning resource. Its potential is limitless but its weakness is the unevenness of the quality of information available. However, it can provide:

- sound files (particularly as these become smaller and easier to download)
- information for projects (particularly for GCSE and A level students)
- information on other music departments (if they publish their websites)
- information from 'official' sites such as the Local Education Authority, Department for Education and Employment, QCA, TTA or OFSTED
- access to professional development resources
- forums for debate and discussion (suitable for teachers and students).

Schools are increasingly developing their own websites and there is great potential for enabling students and parents to have access to information, schemes of work, homework and links to suitable resources.

It might be useful to build up a list of words to include in a web search. For example:

Types of resource	Search words
Government	NGFL, DFEE, TTA, QCA, OFSTED
Resources	MIDI files, sound files, WAV files, MP3 player, MP3 recorder, MP3 files, songs
Associations	Music education organizations, for example *National Association Of Music Educators, Music Education Council, Association of British Choral Directors*
Other users (e.g. *other schools*)	Music lesson plans, music resources, music departments

Useful sites can then be 'bookmarked' and stored in folders on your computer or network. Additionally you may have access to an Intranet service and want to store links to particular pieces of information:

LEA	*Local school websites, advisory services, information databases*

Word processors and desk top publishing

These can be used to write about music. Text can be:

- edited
- re-drafted

- enlarged
- reduced
- centred
- justified
- spell checked.

Pictures can be loaded, adjusted and combined with text. This type of software can be used by staff for the production of resources and used by students for completing and presenting work.

Multimedia authoring

It is possible for students and teachers to write their own multimedia presentations. Various programmes make this possible at a very reasonable price. A presentation might consist of:

- text
- pictures
- sound files
- video clips.

Handled well, this might provide students with a composing stimulus, and may offer the possibility of working across more than one curriculum area. For example, a *group of Year 9 students might work in conjunction with drama to make some music which is used to enhance a media presentation on the use of music in soap operas.*

The music department in the near future

We might expect that music departments in the near future will have:

- between 20 and 30 multimedia computers
- access to the Internet on all of these
- web pages on the school website giving information, homework, parents section, schemes of work and so on
- a range of software to support the development of musical understanding including the requirements of the latest National Curriculum Orders
- other hardware such as keyboards, microphones, recording equipment and sound processors (these will increasingly become integrated with computer technology).

Using ICT effectively

There are many aspects of music teaching where ICT has the potential to be invaluable. As with all resources the actual value will be highly dependent on how skilfully its use is planned. Part of this process will require the teacher to constantly evaluate how effective the particular resource is.

Some good uses of ICT can occur when:

- it enhances musical creativity. For example *students use technology to listen to and manipulate sounds*
- activities are planned against appropriate learning objectives. For example *planning has a clear focus on the intended musical outcome and ICT is used to support this*
- learning is easier or more accessible than when using traditional methods. For example *students with limited performance skills can put an idea into a sequencer slowly, save it and retrieve it for further development*
- students are encouraged to explore, experiment and test hypotheses using sound. For example *students are continually encouraged to develop their aural imagination by giving their greatest attention to the sound of music (rather than its representation on a screen)*
- ICT encourages independence. For example *students are able to find materials on the Internet and utilize them within their essays or compositions.*

Less effective use can occur when:

- the aims and objectives for an activity are not clear. For example *students use ICT because it is there, rather than for a clear musical purpose*
- the use of ICT drives the activity. For example *a sequencer software package results in songs that all have the same 'formula' sound*
- ICT is used as a method for occupying students, or as a reward. For example *it is offered as motivation to students from Year 9 onwards*
- over-emphasis is given to notation (at the expense of what music actually sounds like). For example *GCSE students are asked to use a sequencer to compose a 16-bar melody. They do this in 'step time'. The result is a neat collection of quavers, crotchets and minims which sound uninspired and lack conviction or quality.*

Effective use of ICT includes knowing when it is inappropriate to use it. For example *when students can achieve better results using other resources.*

Getting started

In order to identify how much you utilize ICT and your training requirements you may find the following needs analysis helpful. Tick the appropriate box.

	Total beginner	I use this myself	I have used this in a classroom	I am a confident user and I am clear about how to use this well with students
Recording				
Midi sequencing and Desk Top Publishing				
Keyboards				
Internet				
CD-ROM	·			
Sound processing and recording				
Drill and practice software				

This sort of process will help the teacher to identify his or her training and development needs.

Another approach might concentrate on strengths and areas for further development (see table on next page):

	Use and investigate sounds and structures	Refine and enhance performances and compositions	Extend awareness and knowledge of musical styles
Recording equipment	Strengths: Areas for development:	Strengths: Areas for development:	Strengths: Areas for development:
MIDI and sequencing equipment	Strengths: Areas for development:	Strengths: Areas for development:	Strengths: Areas for development:
Keyboards	Strengths: Areas for development:	Strengths: Areas for development:	Strengths: Areas for development:
CD-ROM	Strengths: Areas for development:	Strengths: Areas for development:	Strengths: Areas for development:
Synthesizers and sound processors	Strengths: Areas for development:	Strengths: Areas for development:	Strengths: Areas for development:

The Internet	Strengths: Areas for development:	Strengths: Areas for development:	Strengths: Areas for development:
Drill and practice software	Strengths: Areas for development:	Strengths: Areas for development:	Strengths: Areas for development:

The outcome will be a list of development priorities. This could be supported by an action plan which sets out how to target the areas identified for development. For more information on self-review see chapter 11.

Three priorities for development:

1.

2.

3.

Summary points:
New technology is causing big changes in society and education. Music education will be affected by these changes. Popular music increasingly makes use of sophisticated technology and students are used to hearing this sort of music on a regular basis. In the future music classrooms are likely to have more computers and have greater access to the Internet.

Integrating the work of the instrumental/vocal teacher

Aim: this chapter examines the role of the instrumental teacher in schools and considers some ways that his or her work can complement and integrate with that of the class teacher.

Music teaching has often exhibited the characteristics of a two tier, or even two class system. On the one hand there are those students who have received extra vocal/instrumental tuition (N.B. it has been assumed that the term instrumental teacher in this chapter includes the work of vocal teachers). Some, although not all, of these will have gained this extra experience within a school. Others will have had private lessons outside a school setting.

> *There remains a gulf in perceptions of school music between the majority who have not had the good fortune to acquire instrumental and music reading skills outside the confines of the classroom, and the minority who have.*
>
> Spencer (1993)

The term 'good fortune' is very revealing, suggesting a negative experience or lack of opportunity for those who do not receive this tuition.

The remainder of students (the large majority) will not receive this tuition and will therefore be reliant upon the teaching experienced in class music lessons. Clearly there is likely to be some disparity between these students and, as noted in chapter 1, it is inevitable that students who have received extra tuition may appear to be more motivated, interested and in-tune with the class teacher's interests. This undoubtedly poses challenges. A possible solution is to ensure that the school caters well for both categories of student.

For example, in a school where this happens *the curriculum caters well for the needs of all students through imaginative, appropriate schemes of work. The music department gives its highest priority to teaching the curriculum and ensures that students with a range of prior experiences and interests are making good progress. There is also a range of out-of-class activities which motivate, engage and stretch students in receipt of extra tuition. Some out-of-class activities are suitable and accessible for all students (including those who have not received extra tuition).*

This is an ideal scenario but requires a considerable investment of staff time and resources. A practical solution might involve visiting teachers assisting with out-of-class activities. This may work well provided that these groups and ensembles are not viewed as high status, whilst 'real' music activities and other things are seen as low status.

The instrumental teacher curriculum

We have already commented upon the potential separateness of the instrumental teaching curriculum. So far we have assumed a philosophy which maintains this separateness but seeks to celebrate and embrace a full range of experience within a school. There might be an even more integrated approach. This has much to commend it. In this scenario:

- instrumental teachers will have access to, and a commitment to, the departmental schemes of work. There will be key points in the year when they will expect to cover certain areas that complement and re-enforce the departmental scheme of work. For example *in Year 8, students study the blues in the first part of the spring term. Instrumental teachers cover the structure of the blues, improvisation, the blues scale, blue notes and listen to examples with their Year 8 students. The students then integrate these skills into their class music lessons*
- instrumental teachers will have copies of the most recent music National Curriculum Orders and examination course requirements. They will expect to make a significant contribution to these areas. Some teachers may be involved in direct teaching of particular classes or groups of students. For example *instrumental teachers with Year 10 and 11 students take responsibility for solo performance, group performance, improvisation and some of the composition activity. This is matched to and complements the work of the class teacher*
- instrumental teachers will have devised schemes of work which complement the National Curriculum Orders, examination requirements and the school's scheme of work.

This scenario may require adjustments to be made in the way that instrumental teachers approach their work. It has implications for:

- initial teacher training
- continuing professional development
- performance management

- Local Education Authorities employing instrumental teachers
- self-employed instrumental teachers.

The changing role of instrumental teachers

In the past an instrumental teacher may have seen their role as one of selecting able students, ensuring they made sufficient progress and inducting them into a range of ensemble opportunities, both in and out of school. This approach is principally derived from the 19th century conservatoire tradition and graded instrumental examinations. There have undoubtedly been changes in this approach. Some change has occurred as a result of market forces introduced into many Local Authority Music Services. For example, *selection may now be an outcome of ability to pay rather than traditional tests of musical ability.* There has also been a growing recognition among today's conservatoires and universities that today's students need a range of skills to cope in the contemporary world of employment. For many this may mean self-employment. The need for this change in approach reflects a society where audiences for classical concerts and sales of recorded performances are falling. In contrast popular music remains buoyant, seemingly able to appeal to its audience with more success. Modern musicians wishing to work principally in a classical style may need to:

- make links with people from a wide age range and variety of backgrounds in order to engage and nurture their audiences
- have effective communication skills
- have confidence in modern technologies such as ICT
- have experience of making music in a range of settings (not just concert halls)
- be well organized and efficient
- develop business and marketing skills
- have good inter-personal skills and be able to communicate with people from a wide range of backgrounds and of differing ages and experience.

Running alongside this there is also a growing realization that instrumental teaching, even at conservatoire level, is not just for those who will become professional musicians. The number of students who will become professional performers is very small. If the function of higher education was merely to train these few, we could greatly reduce the number of places offered. This assumes that:

- we could also significantly reduce the numbers who are offered tuition in the first place

- there was a system in place which had the resources to offer tuition to a selected few and that the level of attainment likely to be achieved by these students was predictable and defined according to clear criteria
- there was an effective selection system which could identify those who were capable of developing into professional musicians.

If, however, higher education is to be more inclusive there will be implications for curriculum organization and how students are taught. This will affect instrumental teachers. If we assume a more inclusive approach, designed to meet the needs of all and equip students for vocational opportunities we might apply the following principles:

- it is not acceptable to just select those who appear to be talented
- instrumental teaching will need to take even more account of the National Curriculum Orders (for example *the inclusion of composing, improvising and appraising music as well as performing*)
- teaching will need to embrace a diversity of musical styles and not just focus on Western classical traditions
- teachers and schools may need to respond much more to the interests of students. This may mean that more teachers of electric guitar, keyboards and drums are required. Offering students opportunities to learn in order to maintain membership levels for the school orchestra or band may be less acceptable than it has been in the past.

Some implications for teaching instrumental lessons

Some of the points have been picked up already in chapter 4 (Differentiation). A good starting point might be to set out a contextual statement:

The National Curriculum Programmes of Study provide frameworks, which can be applied to all musical activities taking place during a school day. These include instrumental teaching and out-of-class activities. Students who receive additional instrumental tuition should receive experiences that develop and broaden their experiences and skills across the full range of the National Curriculum Programmes of Study for music and examination board requirements.

Students receiving traditional extra instrumental tuition have made particular progress in performing pieces, often in a Western classical style and probably from notation. In practice the type of experience will depend on the teacher's background, interests and their approach to lessons. It may be, however, that the student taught in this way is:

- able to read notation quite fluently
- has followed an accredited examination syllabus closely (for example *Associated Board*)
- is experienced in playing within ensembles such as bands or orchestras.

Instrumental examinations have exerted a strong influence on how instrumental teachers approach their work. Most exams include performance of pieces, technical work (such as scales and arpeggios) and aural tests. These are the activities that are found most often in instrumental lessons.

However, students taught in this way may not:

■ be able to play by ear or from memory
■ be able to improvise fluently
■ have listened to music from a wide range of styles and cultures.

In chapter 4 we made a list of those attributes that were required of a complete musician. It follows that if we accept that these attributes are desirable, the instrumental teacher will need to adjust his or her teaching methods in order to ensure the student develops a balanced range of skills. These skills match closely those promoted through the National Curriculum Programmes of Study. Ideally this will happen in conjunction with the class teacher, so that the differing experiences are complementary. An effective instrumental teacher is likely to be able to maintain a balance between these broader skills and the more specific ones required by most instrumental examination schemes.

◢ Teaching aural skills

To play or sing accurately and with expression requires highly developed aural acuity and imagination. Instrumental teachers can make a strong contribution to teaching aural skills. There is a strong argument for always including aural skills as part of the process of learning an instrument. Practising aural 'tests' (such as those required for instrumental grade examinations) may not be the most effective method for developing aural skills in instrumental lessons. This is especially true if the aural test is treated as a separate activity and revised immediately prior to an examination but not developed regularly during other lessons. Consistent development of aural skills through improvisation, performing by ear and from memory as an expectation for most lessons may lead to enhanced aural acuity and awareness among students. An outcome may be that students are subsequently better equipped for success in the aural section of instrumental examinations. Part of this process may also involve regular use of the voice and encouraging students to consider tuning and phrasing preferences. These points also apply to rehearsing and performing in ensembles. Students can often develop their skills in these situations by being asked about tuning, phrasing, tempi or stylistic preferences.

Using a range of styles

In order to produce effective and versatile musicians instrumental teachers should consider a range of areas for their schemes of work and lessons plans. For example, do students:

- encounter a range of musical styles and periods across a year (for example *classical, rock, 'world' music, jazz*)?
- improvise regularly and freely (including tasks set for practice at home)?
- transpose by ear regularly (and understand what transposition is)?
- tune their instruments accurately and make judgements about tuning as part of their performances?
- sing phrases?
- develop short compositions in order to practise a technical problem or develop some other aspect of technique?
- listen critically and with insight to the performances of peers and established professional musicians (in a range of musical styles)?

Selection of students for instrumental lessons

There is a view that music is a talent that some people have and others lack. This view has been commonly held in this country for many years and is particularly prevalent in the context of choosing students who are 'suitable' for instrumental tuition. The amount of this talent is held to be stable (i.e. one does or does not exhibit it in childhood and this talent then remains throughout life). Much of this theory goes back to the work of Francis Galton (1822–1911). Galton proposed that there were inherited traits and he tried to demonstrate this through the lineage of the Bach family. He also developed tests for the trait of intelligence and these served as the model for many later tests of musical ability. However Galton did not take into consideration the shared environment of 'musical' families.

The music testing movement began with Seashore's *Measures of Musical Talents* (1919) and were further developed by several other practitioners. The culmination of these tests were Gordon's test of musical aptitude, Colwell's of achievement and Bentley's test of musical ability. The latter still exerts a strong influence in many schools today. Correlation between the various tests is low, suggesting that there is not a single trait that is being measured. The predictive qualities of the tests (in the sense of likely future success in playing a musical instrument) have proved particularly suspect. Most tests measure aural perception, and these skills are usually exhibited in proportion to the subjects' prior engagement with musical activity. The more you have engaged in music making prior to the test, the better you will do. If there were truly such a thing as musical talent such tests would run the risk of missing it in those individuals with relatively slight prior musical experience, but who never the less have great interest and potential. The tests are also heavily weighted towards music making within the Western classical tradition.

The other intriguing question about these tests is whether they are likely to show a normal distribution across a population. For example:

Is the population likely to be divided into:

highly talented	quite talented	average	very little talent	no talent

If we assume that it is possible to devise a test of musical suitability for learning a musical instrument, which category of talent are we trying to identify? Likely to:

- achieve success as an international soloist?
- work regularly as a principal in an established orchestra?
- work occasionally for ad hoc professional groups?
- achieve grade 8 distinction?
- achieve grade 5 pass?

Common sense tells us that there is no test that is capable of predicting these outcomes. There are too many variables within the equation. However it is still common to find tests applied as if they were predictive and students and parents accepting the result of proof of their suitability to learn an instrument. It is actually far more likely that:

- there is no such thing as musical talent (apart from a very few gifted individuals who have a unique combination of physical attributes, mental attitude and the good fortune to be nurtured at a relatively young age)
- success in playing a musical instrument is in direct proportion to the amount and regularity of practise, the quality of teaching and a supportive and nurturing learning environment
- so called tests of musical ability test prior experience, general levels of educational achievement and are applied in highly idiosyncratic ways.

We can sum up these views in the following way:

Traditional view	Alternative view
Students either have or have not got musical ability.	Anyone can benefit from learning a musical instrument (including those with special needs, English as an additional language and low prior attainment).
This is innate and best assessed through some form of testing process.	Musical skills are learned (although there may be a tiny number with really exceptional talent). We are unlikely to encounter this kind of exceptional aptitude more than once in a career.
Common tests used involve pitch perception, clapping back rhythms or both.	Tests of musical 'ability' give an indication of prior musical experience but tell us relatively little about potential.
Teachers sometimes assess students' 'enthusiasm' or 'attitudes'. They are rarely clear about what this means or how it is assessed.	Boys may not appear to be as enthusiastic or desirable to teach if students are assessed on their attitudes. This may lead to an imbalance of boys and girls learning instruments.

■ Instrumental tuition policies

A school policy on offering instrumental tuition should address the following points:

1. It is helpful to have a brief policy statement on how students gain access to instrumental lessons. If this includes a test, clear information should be given about what the test consists of and why it is being applied. This should make reference to the governors agreed policy on charging. Parents should all have access to this policy (for example *notification in the prospectus that one is available or via the Internet*).
2. If the number of students who wish to learn is the same, or less than the spaces available, all students should automatically be allocated a place. There should be no test of musical aptitude or ability.
3. If the number of applicants exceeds the number of spaces available, clear information needs to be prepared about procedure for allocating spaces (for example *first-come-first-served, a waiting list, availability of*

instruments). This process should be fair, open and even-handed. It is helpful if any policy is contained in the departmental policy or handbook. Due reference ought to be given to the whole-school equal opportunities policy.

4. If it is a condition of receiving tuition that students participate in ensembles, this should be made clear at the outset.

5. If there are alternative means of obtaining tuition, this information should be available (for example *local private teacher, local music centre*).

6. Tuition available should reflect the culture, traditions and interests of the students as well as the school.

7. Equal opportunities and charging are not the same thing. Equal opportunities applies to the full range of ways that students access tuition and includes the selection and availability of tuition. Charging may include an element of equal opportunities but if a charging policy is consistent (i.e. applied to all students fairly) and allows students who are at an agreed level of benefit access this is not likely to be an issue. These areas should be dealt with in the governors' charging policy, and reference should be made to current government legislation and any national or local advice.

8. Under current government legislation individual and group lessons (up to four students) can be charged for.

9. Schools might consider offering free tuition to all students on examination courses.

10. Most tests of 'ability' need careful mediation. In particular, tests of 'enthusiasm' are highly subjective and very difficult to justify. Most standard tests give an indication of prior experience and attainment rather than potential (for example *the Bentley test*). Several tests such as singing back a phrase or recognizing which of two notes is higher have no known link to likely future success in playing an instrument. There is, however, a direct correlation between future 'success' and the amount of time a student spends practising. If a school can help a student to develop good practise routines they will almost certainly be contributing to likely success and enjoyment.

11. The work of the instrumental teacher should be seen as complementary to that of the class teacher. Students who receive instrumental lessons should not be viewed as having higher status than those who have received class music lessons only.

What might this look like in practice?

Example 1

School A is in a rural catchment area. Employment in the area is high and many parents commute to well-paid jobs in a local city. The school scores above average in GCSE and A level results, although is only average compared to similar schools (those with similar entitlement to free school meals). The school employs teachers in:

- voice
- electric and bass guitar
- drums
- upper strings
- lower strings
- brass
- woodwind.

Out of a school population of 1100, 200 students receive tuition. There is no waiting list. Students pay the full cost of tuition (less for group lessons than individual lessons). Twelve students on income support, or other benefits, have their tuition paid for (as set out in the governors' charging policy). Uptake for music GCSE and A level courses is average. The school offers the following out-of-class musical activities:

- band
- orchestra
- junior choir
- senior choir
- keyboard club
- music technology club
- rock school.

The department monitors uptake for these activities, analyses it by gender and has strategies in place to try to improve under-performance by boys. Some of these activities are run by instrumental teachers (many of whom are purchased from the Local Authority Music Service). One instrumental teacher also teaches some aspects of A level and GCSE lessons (this has required some training as part of the department's development plan).

All teachers have copies of the current National Curriculum Orders and examination course requirements (as appropriate). The Head of Music monitors the work of instrumental teachers through a minimum of one lesson observation per year. Additionally, there is communication with parents through the school homework diary (which has a section for instrumental lessons). The class teacher checks on the amount of progress that individual students are making. All staff (including instrumental teachers) meet for a half day conference during the summer term.

Over the next three years the department plans to extend opportunities further by:

- purchasing a Samba kit and running workshops (in conjunction with the Community Education Tutor)
- purchasing a set of steel pans and setting up individual tuition and workshops
- developing further the range of professional musicians used to offer curriculum enhancement.

Example 2

School B is inner city. Examination results are well below the national average but are above average for similar schools (as measured by proportion of students eligible for free school meals). 30% of students are eligible for school meals, and 40% have English as an additional language.

All tuition is subsidized by the school according to an agreed policy. Students in receipt of income support receive free tuition. The school offers tuition in:

- voice (rock and gospel style)
- bass guitar
- electric guitar
- drums
- steel pans
- tabla
- sitar.

Out of a school population of 650, 350 students receive tuition. Uptake for music GCSE and A level courses is well above average.

The school runs the following out-of-class activities:

- gospel choir
- pop choir
- junior and senior Steel pans
- rock and pop workshops.

These activities are all integrated with local community provision and are run during a music school which meets on a Wednesday twilight session.

▨ Things that can be done to ensure greater coherence between the work of the instrumental and class teacher

The class teacher and instrumental teacher can carry out an audit of strengths and weaknesses in order to strengthen links between their work. The following grids can be used as a starting point. A good time to do this might be during the summer term, when some older students are on examination leave.

Joint audit

Area to develop	Strength/area for development	Action to be taken (by whom and when)
Instrumental teachers have a copy of: ■ most recent National Curriculum Orders ■ appropriate examination syllabus ■ relevant school policies ■ departmental handbook ■ departmental schemes of work.		
Identify areas where links can be made and aim to develop one or more of these each year.		
Encourage students to use instruments in class lessons so that they further develop their skills and contribute to the effect and success of compositions and performances.		
Do not make the assumption that students who receive instrumental tuition are more advanced than others. They may lack skills (for example *playing by ear, improvising*).		

Consider ways to improve communication, for example: ■ *a regular meeting time for staff (however brief)* ■ *a note book which is used for communication between class teacher and instrumental teacher* ■ *using the school homework diary for three-way dialogue between class teacher, instrumental teacher and parents.*		
Consider ways in which an instrumental teacher can contribute to an aspect of an examination course or other project. (N.B. this should ideally go beyond demonstrating an instrument or addressing the performance aspect of an examination syllabus). For example *an instrumental teacher may be encouraged to contribute to the full range of the National Curriculum Programmes of Study.*		

Audit for the class teacher

Do I ask students who receive extra tuition to:	Strength/area for development	Action to be taken (by whom and when)
Listen to a piece of music and work out the chord sequence, melody and ostinato pattern etc?		
Learn a melody by ear?		
Add new chords to a melody?		

Learn some strategies to develop playing from memory?		
Develop improvisation skills?		
Develop keyboard harmony skills (for example *playing chords from symbols or abbreviations*)?		
Listen to a rhythm pattern on a keyboard (for example *tango*). Work out the key features of the rhythm or research the rhythm using CD-ROMs or the Internet.		

Audit for the instrumental teacher

Do I ask students who receive extra tuition to:	Strength/area for development	Action to be taken (by who and when)
Transpose?		
Tune their own instruments?		
Use their instruments in class lessons (and find out what they have been doing so that some of this work can be developed still further)		
Do I ensure that teaching embraces the full range of the National Curriculum programmes of study, for example ■ *students perform from notation and by ear/from memory* ■ *encourage students to improvise and compose*		

pieces (perhaps as part of an exercise to cope with particular technical problems) ▪ ensure that students play pieces from a variety of styles and cultures ▪ ensure that students consider the musical effects of different styles, cultures, times and places.		
▪ encourage students to listen to music from a broad range of styles and to consider what gives music its expressive quality, what makes for an effective performance and so on.		

The instrumental teacher will find that nearly all the topics dealt with in other chapters have relevance to their work.

Summary points:
- The work of instrumental and class-based teachers can be strengthened by greater integration.
- The work and training of musicians and instrumental teachers is constantly developing and changing in order to reflect today's society.
- Even today there are many out-dated practices surrounding the selection of students for instrumental lessons.

Effective GCSE teaching

Aim: this chapter considers some of the ways that GCSE music is commonly taught, changes to examination specifications and suggests a more integrated approach.

▨ Introduction

There are many senses in which the GCSE music examination can be considered a success. More students of this age take music examinations than the previous O level and CSE courses combined. This is probably because a wider range of students take GCSE music than took previous examination courses.

However, improvements can still be made. When compared to other optional subjects GCSE music is relatively unpopular. In an average year the proportion of students taking optional examination courses will be:

Subject	% of cohort
Geography	50
History	38
Art and design	38
German	23
Business studies	20
Religious studies	18
Home economics	17
Drama	15
Sports/PE studies	14
Information systems	8
Music	7
Vocational studies	6
Spanish	6
Creative arts	2
Computer studies	2
Dance	1

Girls are significantly more likely to take music than boys.

An outcome of the relatively low numbers taking music is that it appears not to attract a representative sample of students. The average A*–C pass rate and points score for music is above that for most other subjects and suggests that music is attracting a relatively small number of students whose examination results are above average. One might speculate that a significant number of these students will do relatively well in all their examination subjects. Most students opting for GCSE music will probably have done well in music during Key Stage 3. This may reflect a high proportion who have received extra instrumental tuition, which helps them to score high marks in the GCSE music examination. It is equally possible that the process used to select these students for instrumental tuition has favoured those who will generally score well in examinations.

The implications for music education

1. We may need to build still further on the success of GCSE and get better continuity between Key Stage 3 and Key Stage 4 – making sure that music is a realistic option for any Year 9 student, regardless of their prior experience.
2. Making comparisons between the school and national or local A*–C pass rates and points is important. However, there is the potential for relatively large fluctuations in the school's statistics from year to year, particularly because numbers entering the examination are likely to be quite small. It is therefore useful to take a three year average when making these sort of comparisons and to use some kind of 'value added' analysis as well (for example *YELLIS*). For example: *how well did students do in music compared to how well the same students scored in their other subjects?* Similarly it could be useful to track the attainment of GCSE students against their attainment at the end of Key Stage 3.
3. It therefore follows that a 100% A*–C pass rate should not automatically be taken as a sign of success, since these students may actually have under-performed in relation to their experience and capability. Similarly in those schools with a large GCSE entry there is a much greater likelihood of students with a range of prior attainment being entered for the examination, and of results therefore falling below national averages. In this context these results may not be a weakness.
4. Schools should analyse the number of A* obtained and compare this with prior attainment and experience. For example *where most students taking the examination are experienced musicians a 100% A*–C pass rate may represent under-achievement.*

Examination boards provide useful feedback for teachers. For example:

■ examiners' reports contain good information about how to improve students' learning. It is very helpful if this information is shared with students

■ schools usually receive a breakdown of how students scored in the various aspects of the examination course (i.e. the relative performance of students in performing, composing and listening). This provides useful information on how effective the teaching has been. For example *if most students scored less well in the listening component than in the performance component what improvements could be made to the teaching of the listening and appraising components of the examination?*

■ Planning the teaching of GCSE music courses

The organization of the teaching of GCSE courses is often influenced by the structure of the examination specification. GCSE examinations tend to have the following features:

■ performance tasks
■ terminal composing task
■ coursework composing tasks
■ final examination involving listening to musical extracts and writing information about what is heard.

This structure means that these are often treated separately and are used to define lesson activities throughout the two-year course. For example *students do some listening, they compose pieces and they practise performances. These activities are treated separately. Students begin this format at the start of Year 10. They sometimes experience the marking system used for the final GCSE assessment straight away and listen to extracts from past listening papers quite early in the course.* This division of activities is logical and where music is assigned two periods a week the following structure might be used:

■ Period 1 Listening
■ Period 2 Composing.

This structure could be changed for occasional activities, as required. Where there are two teachers in the department, this makes a neat separation for the focus of each teacher:

■ Period 1 Listening (taken by teacher A)
■ Period 2 Composing (taken by teacher B).

Students are asked to find suitable pieces for the performance examination. This might be done in conjunction with the instrumental teacher (although several students may not have an instrumental teacher and may need extra help with this aspect of their coursework).

Medium-term planning

This might result in the following sort of medium-term planning:

Listening lessons (one period per week)	Year 10	Year 11
Autumn	Renaissance Baroque	20th century
Spring	Classical Romantic	Gamelan Revision
Summer	African Indian	Examination

Composing/performing lessons (one period per week)	Year 10	Year 11
Autumn	■ Write an 8–12-bar melody ■ Graphic notation	■ Melody with harmony ■ Free composition
Spring	■ 12-bar blues ■ Atonal music	■ Record compositions ■ Practise performance pieces
Summer	■ Piece for voice ■ Fanfares ■ Performance examination	Listening Examination

See chapter 2 for more information on medium and long-term planning.

In this planning chart listening tasks have mostly been divided chronologically, starting with early music and working towards 20th century examples. Music from around the world is incorporated into the planning in order to give some variety. This process ensures that all students will have encountered these elements and, hopefully, will recognize them if they occur in the listening examination. This method of planning is quite common and has some strengths. The principal one is that it is logical and systematic and should ensure a relatively thorough grounding in knowledge about styles of music linked to musical examples.

It has weaknesses as well. Students listen to musical examples, learn facts about the musical style or culture but **very rarely apply this to their own composing**. Meanwhile composition is treated as a separate activity and pupils are given tasks such as *'compose a melody with between 8 and 12 bars'*. There is very little link between what students are learning about music through listening and the application of this to their own compositions. For example *students might spend one lesson learning about aspects of Renaissance music. They might learn about the use of modes in plainsong or the use of drones and instrumental timbres in dance music. In their next lesson they would then compose a melody but might not use any of the information they have learned about Renaissance music within this process. The two activities run alongside each other but do not link.*

An assumption has probably also been made that composing will focus on producing a composition to fulfil GCSE coursework requirements, rather than being a medium for learning about and understanding music. This is often the case. Students are taught the skills which it is felt are needed to 'pass' the GCSE examination. This might require the completion of two or three compositions. Students work on their compositions over the two-year period but often the style and language used does not develop greatly. This may be because they have not made a link between the music they compose and the music they listen to. A key reason might be because the lessons are taught separately and opportunities for effective links are lost. This is particularly likely if two teachers are taking the course and are teaching separate aspects. This approach can therefore be a quite narrow way of meeting examination requirements, even though it initially seems to be logical. Students may do better if the teaching is more integrated. This can be the case even when students are apparently gaining relatively high A*–C GCSE 'pass' rates. For example *in relation to their prior attainment and capabilities students may be capable of even more.* Even those students who gain A* may be capable of responding to greater musical challenge than a separated lesson structure may allow or encourage.

New examination specifications encourage greater integration between activities.

Integration of activities and ideas

With a more integrated course students will be taught about a wide range of music. They will experience this through:

- developing performance skills

- exploring ideas through composing
- listening to music from different styles, periods and cultures.

Where possible, links will be made between these activities. See chapter 2 for more information on how this idea has implications for medium and long-term planning.

An outcome of this philosophy may be that some pupils know, understand and can do far more than the examination will test. These students may go beyond the requirements for an A*. They should be encouraged to do so. An integrated approach to planning should lead to greater musical understanding and musicians with more developed skills. In chapter 4 we considered the attributes of an effective musician. A definition was used of an effective musician:

- listen to music from a wide variety of styles and cultures
- play by ear and from notation(s)
- communicate expressively using the voice and/or an instrument
- improvise and compose fluently
- listen to music with great insight and aural acuity.

Integrated teaching can help to achieve these aims. It is possible that it may also result in the students scoring more highly in the examination as well.

Long-term planning

In chapter 2 we touched upon some of the points concerning planning across Key Stage 4.

We noted that a GCSE syllabus often contains helpful planning information on the expectations for the listening section. For example:

Pitch	Including scales, modes, intervals
Duration	Rhythms, simple and complex
Dynamics	Differences in volume, changes in volume, accents, articulation
Tempo	Differences in speed, changes in speed
Timbre	Including instrumental sounds, ways in which sound is changed, different qualities of sound
Texture	Density of instrumentation, harmony, polyphony, homophony
Structure	Patterns (for example sequence), phrasing, single idea forms (for example rounds), repetitive forms (for example pop song), developmental forms (for example variation)

In order to achieve integration the teacher might define which of these will be taught during the Key Stage 4 course:

Year 10	Year 11
Pitch (scales, modes, intervals) ■ Minor ninths and use of jazz harmony ■ Plainsong ■ Major/minor scales	**Pitch** (scales, modes, intervals) ■ Jazz modes ■ Whole-tone scale ■ Dodecaphonic music
Duration (rhythms, simple and complex) ■ 5/4 and 7/4 time ■ triplets	**Duration** (rhythms, simple and complex) ■ 3/4 and hemiola ■ dance rhythms – minuet, pavane, mazurka ■ cross rhythms
Dynamics (differences in volume, changes in volume, accents, articulation) ■ use of accents in cross rhythms	
Tempo (differences in speed, changes in speed) ■ creating 'static' effects	
Timbre (including instrumental sounds, ways in which sound is changed, different qualities of sound) ■ using extreme pitches to create effects ■ percussive sounds and sustaining sounds	**Timbre** (including instrumental sounds, ways in which sound is changed, different qualities of sound) ■ using 'special techniques' – muted, col legno, flutter tonguing, glissando
Texture (density of instrumentation, harmony, polyphony, homophony) ■ contrapuntal ideas, fugato	**Texture** (density of instrumentation, harmony, polyphony, homophony) ■ accompaniments – writing for keyboards, arpeggio, patterns
Structure Patterns (for example sequence), phrasing, single idea forms (for example rounds), repetitive forms (for example pop song), developmental forms (for example variation) ■ ternary from ■ binary form ■ variation form	**Structure** Patterns (for example sequence), phrasing, single idea forms (for example rounds), repetitive forms (for example pop song), developmental forms (for example variation) ■ sonata form ■ popular songs ■ free choice

This planning has been set out in this way for two reasons:

1. It matches that used by the teacher for Years 7–9. This helps to give both the teacher and the student a clear sense of progression between Key Stage 3 and Key Stage 4.
2. The examination specification has set out information in this way and it is therefore sensible to make use of this in the teacher's planning.

Other methods of organization and planning may be equally as effective.

The teacher has decided to omit dynamics and tempo from Year 11 because these have been covered in sufficient detail between Years 7 and 10. Some topics will already have been covered. For example *major and minor was a topic in Year 9*. The teacher is happy to revise this because he is clear that the students will be composing, performing and listening to pieces around this concept at a much higher level than in Year 9.

In putting together both medium and long-term planning the teacher has been aware that:

■ composing and listening will be integrated as closely as possible
■ musical examples will be drawn from a wide range of styles, periods and cultures
■ in Year 10, in particular, students will be encouraged to produce a folio of composing ideas or sketches. Some of these may be completed compositions. Some may have the potential to become completed compositions. Sketches may take the form of recorded ideas on tape, written commentaries or use of stave notation. While they are composing students' attention will be drawn to understanding how elements affect the music they listen to and be encouraged to experiment with these ideas when composing.

Students will be encouraged to apply information and understanding gained through listening, appraising and composing to their performances. For example *they will consider the period in which a piece was composed, the structure and significant features of how it was composed and use this information to improve and enhance their own performances.*

Lesson planning

The result of the medium and long-term planning is a scheme of work which is capable of stretching all students in the group. Some of the topics will require differentiated teaching. Short-term planning will need to ensure that all students are challenged but that topics might be broken down into smaller steps for those students who need extra help.

In adopting the above planning approach the teacher has tried to ensure that there is a good link between the music students hear and the music they compose. See chapter 9 for information on how this principle can also be applied to post-16 planning.

Analysis of a set piece or other musical example in order to stimulate composing

Under the long-term planning heading of texture (Year 11) the teacher decides to focus on *contrasting textures (unison and chords)*. He decides that the slow movement of the Beethoven fourth piano concerto provides a good example of this. The piece has several useful features:

- there is a clear structure (which highlights the different textural elements)
- it provides a useful example of part of a concerto
- it offers the opportunity to consider some aspects of classical orchestration and characteristics of the classical period.

The teacher hopes to make maximum use of these opportunities in order to stretch and challenge the students.

He begins by sketching out his own brief analysis of the movement. This helps him to confirm the key features of the piece:

Analysis of piece against musical elements (noting any significant features)
Title *Piano Concerto no.4 in G major*
Composer *Beethoven*
Musical style *Late classical/early romantic period*
Brief description of piece *This is an example of a concerto. A concerto is a piece of music which has one important instrument (in this case the piano) and an orchestra. The orchestra here consists of strings, woodwind, brass and timpani.* *Most concertos from this period have three movements (fast, slow and fast). This is the middle, slow movement. Beethoven wrote five piano concertos. This one was composed around 1806/7.*
PITCH	■ *Use of E minor tonality* ■ *There is much development of melodic ideas (e.g. the dotted motif heard in the strings at bars 1- 5 is developed and changed each time it is heard and the 'chorale-type' phrase heard on the piano in bars 6–13 becomes increasingly fragmented).*

	In the middle section (bars 30–47) diminished seventh chords are used to give harmonic colour and to increase harmonic tension. This gives a sense of loss of harmonic direction, a longing (which may be characteristic of the Romantic period).
DURATION	■ The rhythmic contrast between the dotted, unison opening idea and the legato chords on the piano is a very striking feature. The characterization of melodic/harmonic material in this way is very characteristic of the Romantic period.
TIMBRE	■ The contrast between material is highlighted by the use of contrasting sonorities pianoforte v strings (no woodwind and brass in this movement).
TEXTURE	■ The texture is very significant. **Strings**: unison and staccato. They finally become 'still' at the end of the movement with a last, fading rhythmic gesture from cello/bass bars 64–66. **Piano**: chords and legato. More agitated bars 47–55. It is as if, in a conversation, an argument takes place. The piano has the last word.
DYNAMICS	■ The dynamics follow exactly the concept of a conversation/argument e.g. forte strings answered by quiet pianoforte (molto cantabile).
TEMPO	The tempo is constant and not a feature.
STRUCTURE	The structure is unusual (perhaps reflecting the freer nature of the Romantic period). There are two main ideas that are continuously developed, overlap and which ultimately influence one another. The development of musical material across the movement is likewise characteristic of the Romantic period.
Most important element(s)	In this piece all elements (except tempo) are important. Although it is unusual for all elements to be equally important and so inter-related this may be a reflection of its early Romantic 'style'.
Key features of this piece	A feature of this movement is the interesting use of texture and the extended development of musical ideas across a movement.

Identifying outcomes from the medium-term plan

The teacher has two lessons a week with the GCSE group and students will work with this musical material in both lessons. They will explore ideas through composing and listen to musical extracts (including the slow movement of this piano concerto) in order to deepen their understanding and provide experience of this genre of music. The lessons are designed to draw together different aspects of the course. The teacher intends to take about four weeks (or eight lessons) for this task. Intended learning outcomes are established:

Knowledge	■ knows the common movement structure of a classical concerto ■ knows that pianos were not used in concertos before the classical period (and why) ■ knows the names of three classical composers and some of the historical and social background surrounding concertos
Skills	■ can perform dotted rhythms ■ can perform a legato chord sequence ■ can perform using dynamic contrast to create dramatic effect
Understanding	■ can use contrasted textures to create expressive effect when composing ■ can recognize this feature in Beethoven's 4th piano concerto and other musical examples
Attitudes	■ begins to become familiar with music from the classical period and understands some of the social context in which it was written

The teacher organizes her intended learning outcomes in a very similar way to Years 7–9 and for examination courses post-16. Students are very familiar with this process and it helps them to focus on the key points they need to learn. They are given 'I can do' lists to help them assess their own learning and to set targets (see chapter 2 for more information).

Lesson planning

Some students will not attempt all of the targets set by the teacher. She will expect fewer targets for some students and will break down activities into smaller steps for a few students.

Lesson 1	The class brainstorm ideas about the classical period. They use the Internet and two CD-ROMs to find out information plus some written materials provided by the teacher. The teacher gives them a fact sheet to keep. They listen to several examples of music from the classical period.
Lesson 2	The class are given a composition brief. They are asked to compose a piece of music that uses one solo keyboard or guitar and another group of instruments.

	The group of instruments are to play in unison, with dotted rhythms and forte. This is answered by the solo keyboard instrument which should play chords moving mostly in crotchets, piano. This will create a rhythmic and **textural** contrast.
Lesson 3	The teacher explains that she wants to concentrate in more detail on concertos and piano concertos in particular. The class revise information on this and listen to some examples of concertos from the classical period. Some of these are piano concertos. They also look at concertos from other periods and make decisions about why they belong to a particular period.
Lesson 4	The class carry on with their compositions. They produce, in groups and individually, two contrasting ideas and perform them. They discuss the effect of this contrast. They listen to the slow movement of Beethoven's 4th piano concerto and listen for particular textural effects. They note how this piece uses the idea of contrasting textures. The teacher gets them to focus on the effect that this has on the piece of music.
Lesson 5	They revise the work from the end of the lesson. Taking the Beethoven concerto as a starting point they decide to introduce some refinements into their compositions: They analyse the structure of the piece and how many bars each type of idea plays before being interrupted by the other. For example: *Idea1* — *Idea 2* *Dotted rhythms, orchestra 5 bars* — *Lyrical chords, piano 8 bars* *Dotted rhythms, orchestra 5 bars* — *Lyrical chords, piano 7 bars* *Dotted rhythms, orchestra 3 bars* — *Lyrical chords, piano 2 bars* They also note how the melodic structure of the piece starts to blur as the dotted motif becomes quieter and the pianoforte becomes louder and more agitated. They decide that this idea is very similar to a conversation or argument between two people. They extend their own compositions by incorporating these ideas into their work.
Lesson 6	They work on their compositions and then return to the Beethoven movement for the third time in order to see how else he creates a dramatic effect. They note: ■ the use of odd and even numbers of bars ■ the use of silence at the end of phrases ■ the way melodic ideas are affected by exposure to each other (as if in an argument opinions begin to change)

	■ the use of a free section played by the piano (they understand that this is sometimes called a cadenza).
Lesson 7	Students perform and discuss their compositions. They look at examples of other concertos and note that the use of texture in the Beethoven piece is not typical. The teacher ensures that the students are aware of key, typical features of classical concertos and how they might differ from Baroque, Romantic or 20th century concertos. At this point a link is made between the use of texture in the Beethoven piece and some features of Romantic music. The students discuss how styles change and blur and that one composer can use aspects of more than one style.
Lesson 8	The students are asked to listen to a series of pieces and identify which is a classical concerto and why. They assess their own work and complete some written work on the classical period. Compositions are all either recorded, annotated or written in manuscript form so that they can be used as the basis of a completed composition if required.

At the point where students are ready to listen to the recording of the Beethoven piano concerto slow movement the teacher gets them to fill in a blank version of the analysis sheet she started with:

Analysis of piece against musical elements (noting any significant features)	
Title *Piano Concerto no.4 in G major*	
Composer *Beethoven*	
Musical style	
Brief description of piece	
PITCH	
DURATION	

TIMBRE	
TEXTURE	
DYNAMICS	
TEMPO	
STRUCTURE	
Most important element(s)	
Key features of this piece	

This helps them to organize their listening so that they focus on key elements in the piece. They are encouraged to use this technique regularly during the course. When they take the terminal listening examination they find this has helped them to listen to pieces in an effective way. It also helped to add creativity and depth to their compositions.

What are the key features of this way of working?

■ students are encountering 'real' pieces of music that they relate directly to their own compositions

■ students' composing activities encourage them to make use of a wide range of ideas (and do not always require a completed composition). This helps them to experiment, take occasional risks and develops their sense of musical language

■ the teacher keeps the focus on what creates a musical effect. For example *the students do not just listen to a recording and note that it is an example of a concerto, a slow movement, or of a piece from the late classical/early Romantic period. They consider the structure of the Beethoven slow movement and consider how a musical effect is achieved. They have the opportunity to try to explore a similar musical effect in their own compositions*

■ these principles can be applied to any piece of music, in any style and used as a stimulus for deepening understanding and developing compositions

■ GCSE music specifications increasingly require integration of activities.

Summary points:

■ It is not always helpful to have one lesson, or part of a lesson, dedicated to one component of the GCSE examination without considering how activities can be integrated as much as possible.

■ A useful starting point for composing activities is often a piece of music – taking the key features of the piece and using these as a stimulus to develop the student's understanding.

■ Successful GCSE teaching is likely to consist of far more than meeting minimum examination requirements.

Effective teaching of post-16 examination courses

> **Aim:** this chapter sets out some of the ways that the teaching of examination courses for students aged 16+ can be taught effectively. An approach is proposed which encourages integration of activities.

◤ Examination courses within the post-16 curriculum

Post-16 courses have been through recent revisions. These have aimed to:

- encourage students to take a wider range of subjects (in order to broaden their curriculum experience)
- address the parity of esteem between A levels and other accredited courses (such as GNVQ) and encourage students to consider mixing the types of accreditation they opt for
- preserve a sense of quality within A level courses.

There is tension between the first two points and the third. A levels are, quite rightly, held in high esteem by some employers and higher education institutions. However, there is also a growing realization that in this country students specialize, and therefore narrow their studies, at a relatively early age. There is some merit in studying a wider range of subjects for a longer period of time and commentators have pointed to other European countries as an example of how this might be put into practice. This is allied with the need for:

- qualifications with vocational relevance
- attracting into higher education students for whom A level courses are not appropriate, or attractive.

Some students will find current A level music courses too theoretical and would welcome an alternative more directly related to the world of employment. It is important that vocational qualifications are seen to have a parity of esteem with more traditional examination courses, so that they do not risk becoming unpopular as a result of perceived low status. These tensions are not unique to music education.

At present music, along with any other subject, can be taken by students as an A level (AS plus A2). It is also available as a short course (AS). The Qualifications and Curriculum Authority (QCA) have defined national criteria, which all specifications have to meet. Music can also contribute to other accredited examinations, such as GNVQ Performing Arts, and there is a discrete A level Music Technology examination. The hope is that the new flexibility introduced into the sixth form will cause more students to consider taking music as an examination course beyond the age of 16. There are two main factors that will affect what happens:

1. How well schools are able to support the relatively few students who may opt for music courses (unless the school is able to enter into a consortium arrangement with other schools). Evidence from past A level courses suggests that schools have been willing to support minority subjects such as music because they are considered to be important and are awarded a relatively high status.
2. Whether post-16 courses are flexible enough to attract a wider range of students than present A level courses (for example *by including popular, jazz and world music options*), while still providing a sufficiently specialized course for those with a more 'traditional' approach.

These are similar to the difficulties that surrounded the introduction of the GCSE music course. We noted in chapter 1 that there were some early fears about the negative impact that GCSE would have on standards. These fears have generally been overcome, and additionally GCSE music does now attract significantly more students than the O level and CSE courses combined. Hopefully this can be replicated in the development of post-16 courses.

What does an examiner look for?

All examination boards publish an annual report on how students fared in particular aspects of the examination. The information in these reports provides an extremely useful planning aid. It is often, although not always, studied closely by the teacher. Where this happens, it contributes to teaching which is focused well on examination requirements. The information contained in examiners' reports is sometimes shared with students. This is a strength, since it may help them to improve their examination technique and achieve a better result. Occasionally the teacher will share general information about the examiner's report with students.

This is helpful. It may be even more helpful to give students actual copies of the report, or make the information it contains readily available. Similarly some teachers provide good information about the examination syllabus. Students may be given copies of the syllabus or a breakdown of the content, a sort of brief synopsis. All examination syllabuses contain lots of useful information and even if students do not have their own copy it is helpful if they have easy access to one. For example:

In section B, candidates are required to answer one question about one of the prescribed works they have studied. At this level it is not expected that candidates will be familiar with the intricate techniques of musical analysis. They should, however, be able to explain the overall structure of a movement or section; show how themes are related to one another (or not, as the case may be); distinguish between the introduction of new material and the continuation or extension of old; understand the key structure of the music and the influence this had on its form. The examiners will be looking for evidence that candidates have listened widely and intelligently and are genuinely familiar with the music they write about.

This brief extract from a specification gives a wealth of information, which any student would find very useful. It is helpful if the teacher can draw the students' attention to this, and many other helpful passages. For example:

The teacher might draw students' attention to the relevant part of the specification. Having done so it would then be useful to ask the students to:

- *explain the overall structure of the movement in question*
- *demonstrate how the themes in movements one and three are related to each other.*

This may help them to bring a focus to their work and encourage them to explore some of these ideas on their own.

Examination specifications

Each specification is different and individual choices will need to be made about which is most appropriate for a particular group of students. A lot will depend on their interests and experiences. All specifications have certain activities in common:

Essay writing or topic/project
Students will try to demonstrate:

- a clear understanding of a piece(s)
- reference to a cultural context (probably through other related works)
- a style of writing which sets out information in a lucid, logical and organized way

■ evidence that the student has some kind of aesthetic or emotional engagement with the piece.

This has two implications:

1. Biographical information about composers is unlikely to score highly or impress, unless it is used to illustrate well a point about a cultural context. For example *information about when Beethoven lived, died and wrote his symphonies may be useful if it enables the writer to make a telling point about how style has changed over time, why a particular piece is radical or innovative or how this work relates to other contemporary ideas. On its own it tells very little.* It is still common to find some students dealing with factual information about music in an uncritical way and rarely being encouraged to apply it effectively.

2. A standard analysis from a book, periodical or magazine regurgitated in an examination will almost certainly be recognized by an examiner. The teacher needs to consider these analyses but in a critical way. The student needs to be encouraged to consider his or her own response to a particular piece and how to communicate this effectively. This is not easy and requires careful planning and skilful teaching.

An effective teacher will need to consider how successful his teaching programme has been in order to adjust and improve upon it. For example:

■ *if students are not able to sufficiently consider their own response to a piece and communicate this effectively, how can the teaching be modified and improved in order to help them?*
■ *what does an analysis of how students fared in various parts of the examination tell the teacher about how effective teaching has been?*

Aural skills

Aural skills can be demonstrated through tests of aural perception, performance on an instrument and perceptive comments about what a student hears when listening to a set work. All these skills need to be developed. For example *practising past A level type aural test papers may do little to develop these skills, especially if students are introduced to past papers too early.* Aural skills need to be nurtured and developed. Even working through a gradated system of aural tests (for example *starting with easier ideas and building up to more complex ones*) may not achieve the desired result. This also applies to the indiscriminate use of published materials designed for post-16 examination courses.

When performing, music students should be constantly encouraged to develop their aural acuity. There are a number of ways this can be done:

- ensuring that students regularly improvise and play by ear as part of their coursework and instrumental lessons. This skill may not be specifically required for the examination but may make a strong contribution to effective aural skills – which are part of the terminal exam. For example *a very good teacher may not restrict her activities to those defined in examination specifications. Her approach may be far more imaginative, and therefore more effective.* This method of working may require dialogue and negotiation with the instrumental/vocal teacher, who may not be initially sympathetic to this approach
- when students are involved in rehearsals for ensembles such as chamber groups, bands, orchestras or choirs they can be asked to state preferences about tempi, phrasing or dynamics. This will encourage them to become more astute listeners. This is a challenging task for the teacher, who may need to occasionally admit that the students' suggestions are superior. Handled well this can be very powerful. It helps students to feel that their opinion is valued. The teacher will need to feel self-confident enough to discuss points with them. There will be some agreement and disagreement. This is healthy
- it may be useful to build some regular singing into coursework. This can be individual, or as part of a small group. The latter is probably preferable since it often requires the ability to listen carefully to other singers and respond effectively. Much will depend on how many students are in a particular group. This activity may do a lot to develop their ability to 'hear' music effectively. It is helpful to include some coaching on how to sing well, so that it encourages them to feel a strong sense of achievement. Improvisation and singing music from a range of styles can also be included as part of this activity. Students can be encouraged to consider the style of the music and relate it, where appropriate, to music they are studying for set works. For example *if they are studying the masses of Palestrina they might sing some extracts and talk about the melodic balance, shape and flow. They could then sing other settings of a mass and compare the musical style. They could then compose settings of the mass using stylistic ideas taken from the music of Palestrina. They could sing these, relate them to the works studied and be encouraged to deepen their understanding through making effective links between the activities.*

Performing skills

Performing skills should be integrated into all other activities. In lessons and in ensemble rehearsals students should be developing:

- **analytical skills:** *for example considering the structure or other musical features of the pieces they are playing. Relating them to a historical or cultural context*

- **aural skills:** *for example working on tuning and phrasing during rehearsals and in performance*
- **making links with their own compositions:** *for example in their instrumental lessons using musical material to develop and extend compositions. This might be done in conjunction with the study of set works. For example if students are studying a classical concerto they might be able to consider examples of this genre with their instrumental teacher. This could include listening to recordings, performing pieces, analysing sections and taking related ideas as a stimulus for composition.*

Composing skills

Composing is an extremely useful activity, as well as a potential musical outcome. Even those students who elect not to take composition coursework can compose in order to deepen their understanding. For example *they can take key features of pieces of music they study and explore these through composition. This process will help their musical understanding and may improve the quality of their analysis or essay writing.* Some examples are given at the end of this chapter.

Post-16 courses will increasingly be expected to make a contribution to students' Key Skills. The post-16 scheme of work should include information on how these will be taught.

Effective post-16 teaching

Effective teaching of post-16 examination courses has some key features. What is taught as part of an examination course may go far beyond what is specifically required for the examination. A course that merely covers the requirements of an examination syllabus is likely to have some limitations. Broadening the scope of students' experience is important. It is also likely that this approach will ultimately enable them to score even higher marks in their examination.

For example *as part of their aural training students may be encouraged to improvise in a jazz style. They might learn about guide tones, voice leading and use of ninth and eleventh chords. Students may use this technique to enrich the harmonic language of their compositions. They make links between the music they compose, listen to and perform. This occurs because the teacher planned it within her scheme of work, and ensured that the students were introduced to musical ideas that went beyond syllabus requirements.*

It is essential to have a scheme of work for post-16 students. This scheme should be shared with them at the start of the course. **Even when there is only one student**. It will offer some distinct advantages:

■ it should ensure that activities are integrated in a more effective and meaningful way

■ it will ensure that an ambitious and rich diet of musical skills and information is covered. Students will value this and find it useful

■ the scheme can be used to provide information for students about areas they will study. This can empower them to carry out their own research and gradually become more independent of the teacher (skills that will be useful for higher education and future employment).

Examples of integrating activities as part of a post-16 course

In the following examples, links are made between specific pieces of music and activities such as composing. The intention is to:

■ promote a deeper understanding of set-works, by exploration of ideas through composing tasks

■ enrich harmonic and structural language in compositions by study of relevant composers and application of key elements which are expressive.

In each case, key elements have been picked out from pieces of music. The objective has been to:

■ give these elements a clear, expressive focus which illuminates the way a particular piece works

■ demonstrate how they can be used to provide a stimulus for composing activity

■ encourage students to relate the outcomes of their composing back to the solutions applied by the composer in question.

This principle can be applied to any piece of music.

The teacher, and ultimately the student, will need to decide on the key features of a particular piece. The key features are those elements or facets of a piece which have a powerful and important musical effect. Each piece will have a different key feature and different commentators may value different key features from the same piece. It is important to discuss this with the students. Choosing the key features helps to encourage an emotional engagement with a piece, rather than a technical description. A useful way to start this process can be to carry out an analysis using musical elements as a template. This requires relative judgements to be made about why a piece achieves a particular effect.

The following proforma could be used:

Analysis of piece against musical elements (noting any significant features)	
Title	
Composer	
Composition date	
Other contemporary pieces	
Musical style	
Brief description of piece	
PITCH	
DURATION	
TIMBRE	
TEXTURE	
DYNAMICS	
TEMPO	
STRUCTURE	
Most important element(s)	
Key features of this piece	

Once completed, this proforma can be useful for the student as a revision resource.

Using pieces of music as a stimulus for composing

In chapter 8 a plan was given of how to use a piece (Beethoven Piano Concerto No. 4) as a stimulus for integrating activities and developing composing. The general principle applied is:

1. Analyse a piece and decide on some key features.
2. Use these as a basis for composing activities.
3. Ask students to relate their own ideas to the original source.
4. Explore ideas in greater depth.
5. Test and develop understanding through written work, listening and further composing activities.

Applying the principles to post-16 courses

Example 1: Beethoven Symphony number one in C major 1st movement (introduction)
The teacher will need to decide on the key feature of this piece (for example *what makes it musical, what is its cultural context and what is likely to make the listener engage with it?*) There may be different views about this.

The teacher decides that a key feature of this piece is: *contemporary development of sonata form, particularly the structural possibilities of tonality. This involves setting up a sense of tonality, shifting away from it and then achieving a sense of equilibrium and release through a return to the original tonality once more.*

The teacher therefore notes down the following points:

Analysis of piece against musical elements (noting any significant features)
Title *Symphony number one in C major 1st movement (introduction)*
Composer *Beethoven*
Composition date *First performed 1800 (probably written 1799)*
Other contemporary pieces *Other composers who wrote music in the 'classical style' Mozart (e.g. Symphony No. 41 Jupiter) or Haydn (e.g. Symphony No. 104 London). The Haydn piece also has a slow movement at the start of the first movement. Mozart and Haydn both developed the use of sonata form in their symphonies and in other pieces as well. Beethoven's music is often seen as a link between Classical and Romantic styles.*
Musical style *The piece is in four movements:*

1) *Allegro con brio (with slow introduction – adagio molto)*
2) *Andante cantabile con molto*
3) *Menuetto – Allegro molto e vivace*
4) *Adagio – Allegro molto e vivace*

Brief description of piece

Contemporary development of sonata form focused on the structural possibilities of tonality. This involves setting up a sense of tonality, moving away from it and then achieving a sense of equilibrium and release through returning to the original tonality once more. In this piece the structural development of tonality seems to be very important.

The introduction achieves this effect by setting up confusion about the tonal centre from the outset. The first chord of C7 implies a tonal centre of F major. The series of dominant seventh chords which follow constantly play with the listener's sense of tonality, finally leading to a resolution into the tonic of C major at bar 13 (the start of the allegro).

PITCH	The introduction consists of a series of musical fragments – there are no developed themes. Melodic ideas are related to specific chords (e.g. the violin part in bars 6 to 8 hovers around the chord of G major (in this case establishing a dominant preparation for the tonal centre of C major) Use is made of dominant sevenths to establish tonality (e.g. bars 1 to 4). Use is made of inversions, perhaps destabilizing any implied sense of tonality (e.g. bars 5 to 7 V, V7d, Ib, Vb).
DURATION	The use of rhythm is not a strong feature of the introduction – it becomes a stronger feature in the allegro that follows.
TIMBRE	Effective use is made of the tone colours of woodwind, brass and strings. For example: Bars 1–3 strings play pizzicato against the woodwind held chords (which are marked fp). This gives a particular quality to the music, which seems playful, and helps to underline the sense of the tonality not being strongly established but only transient. The use of arco strings and brass at the start of bar 4 gives emphasis to the chord of G major (used here as a dominant for the tonality of C major). This helps to establish this chord as being important (compared to the opening chords which are more transient).
TEXTURE	The texture is principally homophonic.
DYNAMICS	Dynamics are constantly used to emphasize and reinforce structural effects. For example: The opening chords begin forte but resolve on to a piano. This destabilizes their harmonic direction and ensures that a strong tonal centre is not established. In bars 8–12 the introduction begins to reach a climax as the desired tonal centre of C major finally becomes established. Forte, tenuto chords seem to reinforce this. The resolution is enhanced further by the

	fact that the final dominant chord is piano (preparing the way for the tutti, forte start of the allegro).
TEMPO	*There is one tempo in this piece.*
STRUCTURE	*The structure of the introduction is not an important feature, although the structure of the first movement and the use of sonata form is a key feature. The introduction may be seen as a preparation for the harmonic structure of the first movement.*
Most important element(s)	*Pitch, timbre and dynamics are used within a strong structural framework*
Key features of this piece	*Contemporary development of sonata form, particularly the structural possibilities of tonality. This involves setting up a sense of tonality, shifting away from it and then achieving a sense of equilibrium and release through a return to the original tonality once more.*

There may be different views about what is significant in this piece. Any views which can be justified are acceptable and it is important that students are taught to view ideas critically. In order for the students to move beyond a technical description of chords, cadences and structure they will need to begin to engage with the music, to feel its special qualities and to bring to bear some personal preferences. This analysis will start to alert them to some of the things that may make this particular piece 'work'. We can see that the harmonic language, dynamics and timbre are particularly important. They are also linked. Very few conventional analyses will make this point. This is the sort of engagement with a piece an examiner will look for.

Using a standard analysis from a text book or periodical

An analysis from published sources will be of interest to students. For example:

> I am delighted to find myself anticipated by Mr. Vaclav Talich in the view that the opening is mysterious and groping, and that the first grand note of triumph is sounded when the dominant is reached.
>
> The first theme of the allegro con brio is a quietly energetic, business-like proposition, moving in sequences from tonic to super-tonic, and thence rising through subdominant to dominant. It is the opening of a formal rather than a big work.

(Tovey 1972: 22/23)

This passage raises some interesting questions and it might be helpful to establish with students that these sources of musical analysis can be treated as an area for investigation, rather than automatically accepted verbatim. For example in this case:

- how is the opening 'mysterious'?
- why is a 'grand note of triumph' reached when the dominant is reached?
- why is it the opening of a 'formal rather than a big work'?

Students can be asked to assess how Tovey's statements of opinion are supported with direct evidence from the piece of music. When considering the work of other writers, students can be asked to consider how much of what is presented is either factual information (with little emotional engagement) or speculative opinion (not supported by evidence). They may find it helpful to reflect on this in order to inform their own analysis technique. A useful exercise might involve encouraging students to consider a passage such as that by Tovey and asking questions such as:

- how much of this is personal opinion?
- how far are opinions supported by evidence?
- where there are two writers describing a piece how far do their views match?
- in what ways is a writer such as Tovey influenced by contemporary views about music and its cultural context (for example *asking the students to use the text as source material but treating its content with some caution*)?

Using other sources

Equally students could consider critically other sources and perhaps draw comparisons about a piece by comparing different writers' views, for example, from information found on the Internet or on a CD-ROM:

Ludwig van Beethoven (1770–1827)

Background

Beethoven was born in Bonn, Germany and was one of seven children in the family, four of whom died at infancy. He inherited his musical talent from his grandfather, Louis van Beethoven, who was employed at the court of the Elector of Cologne. Louis was a capable musician and eventually became the Elector's Director of Music. Beethoven's father, Johann, was also employed there as a musician but had limited talent and a very aggressive personality. Johann drank excessively, was constantly chasing after women and was very cruel to Ludwig. He did, however, realize Ludwig's potential, but was disappointed when his son,

---

who developed his talents slowly, did not become a child prodigy like Mozart. It was his deeply loved mother, Maria Magdalena, who kept order within the household by attempting to control Johann's excesses.

Emotional freedom
Beethoven's style is an important bridge between Classicism and the new Romantic style. His music, particularly from his middle and late periods, has an emotional intensity and drama that cannot be found in middle Classical works by Haydn and Mozart.

Form
Beethoven usually adhered to strict Classical forms, but often introduced daring new structures (i.e. the finale of the 9th Symphony and the late string quartets).

Orchestration
Beethoven was the first composer to fully utilize the possibilities of the modern symphony orchestra.

This passage raises some important points. The teacher might encourage students to question the validity of some of the statements. For example:

'His music, particularly from his middle and late periods, has an emotional intensity and drama that cannot be found in middle Classical works by Haydn and Mozart.'

- how do we know this?
- what, if any, examples can we use to illustrate this point?

'Beethoven was the first composer to fully utilize the possibilities of the modern symphony orchestra.'

- what does this statement mean?
- what do we understand by 'the modern symphony orchestra'?
- give some examples of how Beethoven utilized it (and why Haydn or Mozart did not).

It may be helpful to ask students to research ideas using a range of media (for example *Internet, CD-ROM, text books*) and compare the information they obtain. For example:

- what is a symphony?
- what is sonata form and how does it work?
- how does this piece relate to the remainder of Beethoven's output?
- how does this piece relate to the work of other contemporary composers?

All these questions will be inter-related. More information is given in chapter 10 on ways that students can pursue these questions in even greater depth.

Using a set piece as a stimulus for further exploration

Having used the introduction to Beethoven's 1st symphony as an initial stimulus, the teacher may decide to explore ideas in greater depth. The teacher might want to provide students with a context for the piece:

The piece starts with a slow introduction. This is unusual but there are several other precedents. *(Ask students to research some and compare them with this piece)*. The whole of the introduction can be viewed in terms of establishing a tonal centre (in this case C major). It achieves this through a series of playful gestures. For example, the first chord is the dominant seventh of F major (rather than the C major tonality of the piece). *What is the effect?* It might be described as humorous, in a deliberately clumsy way. *Why does it sound 'clumsy'.* A dominant seventh is one of the clearest ways there is for establishing a sense of tonality. *(Ask students why this is and to find some other examples)*. Starting the piece with this chord (followed by a resolution) is drawing attention to the movement's preoccupation with tonality. It is as if the composer is posing the question 'just what key is this piece of music in?' Is this what Tovey means by 'groping'. It is perhaps harder to justify it as 'mysterious'. *(Ask students what they think Tovey meant by this term)*.

Further examination of the introduction reveals a series of features, which appear to reinforce this notion:

- there are a series of dominant seventh chords which resolve at the fourth bar onto a chord of G major (the dominant of the actual tonality of the piece). These chords seem to keep the listener guessing about the final tonal centre of the piece, since a dominant seventh is a defining tonal chord but the constant shifting of tonal centre has a destabilizing effect
- any sense of tonality at bar 4 (G major, dominant of C) is immediately undermined by the use of chromatic notes such as G#. This might be described as characteristic of a playful approach to the tonal stability of the piece and one of the ways the composer keeps the listener guessing about future direction
- bars 5 and 6 begin to establish the sense of G major (as a dominant to C major) through the use of G7 in bar 5, the use of 1b (in C major) in bar 6 and V7b in bar 6. However, each of these is destabilized by the use of chromatic notes.
- the use of forte and piano dynamics in bars 8–11, the use of silence and a series of cadences increases the tonal tension further. By now the listener is ready to reach the resolution to this tension

■ bar 12 provides the required implied dominant seventh in the sustained woodwind chord. The strings continue the sense of tonal ambiguity to the last by the use of an ascending F# and descending F natural

■ the resolution, when it comes is welcome. The allegro con brio begins with full orchestra (but piano). The dynamics can be related very effectively throughout to the sense of tonal direction and conflict.

Note the melody part at the allegro. The use of the tonic, dominant and leading note in a melody is almost a parody of the type of melody, which is clearly in one particular key. This replicates the playful, humorous nature of the piece to date. This nature is further confirmed by the sequential shift of the melody into the super-tonic (just at the moment when the key centre appears to be unassailable).

Choosing composition activities from this stimulus

Having established a rationale for this movement, it can be used to help students explore and understand the music further. This is where composing can be very effective. This is so even if students have not elected to take composition as part of the terminal examination. Students can explore ideas through composing, in order to come to a better understanding of how a piece works. The resulting **composition** is less important than the process of exploring ideas by **composing**.

For example in relation to the Beethoven 1st Symphony (introduction) students could be asked to:

1. Compose a piece of music which is in one key but which has an introduction in a different key. The piece should have a slow introduction.
2. The introduction should lead the listener to want the sense of key to be resolved and use various ways of leading the listener to expect one key while actually being led to another.
3. Reinforce these tonal effects through the use of dynamics.
4. Once a faster section has been reached, write a melody which implies a clear sense of tonal centre. What features will the melody have in order to do this?
5. Make best use of the timbral qualities of strings, woodwind, brass and percussion to enhance the tonal effect you require. This could be achieved using ICT resources.

Applying the principle to other pieces of music

Example 2: Byrd four part mass Agnus Dei
This is a difficult piece to approach because the sound world used by composers like Byrd is very specialized, and probably more removed from

the experience of most students than orchestral music. To an expert the difference between the harmonic language of Tallis and Byrd is enormous, but to a novice listener they can sound very similar. It is often helpful when considering key features to consider some of the broader structural issues first. We might start by helping the students to consider how the piece works in relation to the musical elements. This will hopefully give them a good overview of the piece and begin to draw their attention to some of its key features.

Analysis of piece against musical elements (noting any significant features)	
Title *Mass for four voices (Agnus Dei)*	
Composer *William Byrd*	
Composition date *Circa 1590*	
Other contemporary pieces *Church music by Gibbons, Tomkins, Philips, Tallis (in England) and Palestrina, Lasso and Victoria on the continent.*	
Musical style *This piece uses a mixture of polyphonic and homophonic ideas. Byrd's masses are unique among contemporary English music in the use of the ordinary of the Latin Mass (reflecting the Catholic faith in a Protestant country). Imitation between parts is common but there is very little use of counterpoint (compare this for example with the work of Palestrina).*	
Brief description of piece *The Agnus Dei is the last part of the mass. In a service the words are commonly repeated three times.* *Agnus Dei qui tollis peccata mundi, miserere nobis* *Agnus Dei qui tollis peccata mundi, miserere nobis* *Agnus Dei qui tollis peccata mundi, miserere nobis* *This is how Byrd treats the words(no doubt reflecting on the spiritual significance of the number 3), with a final section:* *Donna nobos pacem* *Musically this is treated as a separate section*	
PITCH	*The music is set freely with ideas which influence other parts but which are rarely repeated exactly. Ideas often develop into more elaborate versions as they are taken over by a new part. The sections of the movement have a unity of style but no common material is used in each section.*
DURATION	*The rhythmic impetus of the piece is extremely free. In modern editions this movement is sometimes barred in four beats to the bar. This*

	facilitates reading the score but risks losing the freedom of the individual part writing as stresses are placed within a conventional time signature.
TIMBRE	*Not a feature for this piece.*
TEXTURE	*Texture is extremely important in this movement.* *The three sections are treated differently (see structure) and this creates a great sense of contrast between them. This textural contrast is carried through into the final donna nobis pacem where all four parts are used together (creating a much thicker texture).*
DYNAMICS	*There are no dynamic markings.*
TEMPO	*There is one tempo (therefore not a strong feature in this piece)*
STRUCTURE	*The structure is very important. See the points about texture above. The structure is very clearly defined and clearly used as a way of creating expressive effect.* *First setting (12 bars)*: Two part texture, use of imitation between the parts.* *Second setting (15 bars): Three part texture, similar use of imitative ideas.* *Third setting (13 bars): Four part texture, continued use of imitation.* *Donna nobis pacem (18 bars): change of musical material, use of dissonance and imitation.* **The bar numbers are taken from the edition edited for modern use by Henry Washington and some useful discussion can take place about the desirability of trying to group this kind of music into regular barring patterns.*
Most important element(s)	*The use of imitation (pitch) and texture are important. This is reflected in the structure, which reflects the structure provided by the text.*
Key features of this piece	*The piece seems to build up emotional intensity through the way the sections are set using a different texture. The culmination of this is the final section, and the words donna nobis pacem, which achieves a strong emotional intensity.*

Clearly this piece does not work within the same kind of larger scale tonal structures encountered in a work like the Beethoven symphony. Going through the analysis process should begin to give the students some clues about how the piece works:

- Byrd clearly varies the texture in order to highlight the threefold nature of the word repetition
- there is a perceptible emotional intensity to the *donna nobis pacem* section. The link with the words is clearly no accident. It would be worth investigating this section further in order to analyse how Byrd achieves this effect.

Similarly students could interrogate, in a critical manner, standard texts about this piece.

> *He was the last great composer in the rich tradition of Catholic polyphony in Britain and the first of that 'golden age of music' which began in the middle years of Elizabeth I's reign. His Latin church music embodies the final perfect union between the native tradition and the contrapuntal techniques that flourished in Italy and the Netherlands earlier in the century.*

(Brown 1976: 327)

For example:

- in what way does Byrd's music embody the perfect union between the native tradition and the contrapuntal techniques that flourished in Italy and the Netherlands?
- what was the native tradition?
- who were the composers writing in Italy and the Netherlands?
- what style did they use?
- how did this compare with Byrd?
- how typical was Byrd's music of contemporary English style?

> *It is difficult to imagine too, circumstances that would have been appropriate for performances of Byrd's three settings of the Mass Ordinary, compositions that survive only in copies with their pages missing, perhaps significantly, so that we do not know the year they were published (though a case can be made for supposing they came out between 1592 and 1596). Byrd's Masses for three, four and five voices are all free of borrowed material or any scaffolding devices, although they do make limited use of head motifs. Byrd built up these magnificent structures from imitative polyphony handled freely and flexibly in his finest mature manner. But his Masses are literally incomparable, for no continental composers invented a textural complexity quite the same as that which characterizes Byrd's music as English, and no other British composers of his generation wrote polyphonic settings of the Ordinary of the Mass.*

(Brown 1976: 328/9)

- what is meant by the term 'scaffolding device'?
- what is a 'head motif'?
- who else used one?
- did Byrd use a 'head motif' in other compositions?
- in what way is the imitative polyphony handled 'freely and flexibly'?
- how did Byrd's music demonstrate textural complexity and compared to whom?

Having carried this analysis students might be asked to carry out a composition task:

Compose a piece for four voices (SATB), setting the words Agnus Dei qui tollis peccata mundi (set three times), Donna nobis pacem. Each section should be treated differently: for example two part, three part or four part texture. The last section (Donna nobis pacem) should represent the climax of the piece. Think carefully about the meaning of the words and how to express this in the music. Use imitation in the music.

Summary points:

Post-16 examination courses may consist of far more than is suggested by a particular specification. Activities should be integrated in order to deepen students' understanding. Aural skills can be taught as part of any activity. Students should be encouraged to become increasingly independent performers who are able to make their own decisions about music. When writing about music students should be encouraged to:

- achieve clarity
- demonstrate that they have listened to and engaged with the music
- support an argument with evidence.

10

Making a contribution to the whole school

> **Aim:** this chapter sets music education within the context of the whole school. An examination is made of music's unique place within the curriculum and how it can contribute to other aspects of a student's development.

◼ The place of music within schools

About ten years ago one might have been able to find examples of a music department like this:

The music department appears to be removed from other areas of school life. It has literally been removed by being placed as far away as possible (in order to minimize the impact of noise on the rest of the school). There are two music teachers. One is an experienced head of department who has been in post for 26 years. The other is a newly qualified teacher who has been appointed in order to modernize and update the department. The department has sometimes resisted initiatives introduced into other subjects. Assessment has been problematic. One reason for this is that the music teachers at the school have often been elsewhere when whole-school decisions are taken, since they have given very generously of their time when running out-of-class activities. The school has a good reputation for music in the local community. The department employs a range of instrumental teachers. They do not have the chance to meet members of staff outside the music department and receive no information about other activities in the school. To all intents and purposes they are outsiders paying an occasional visit.

There are very few departments like this today. This example is presented because it highlights important points about some of the ways that music can miss opportunities to relate to the life of a school and its community. Even today it seems quite rare for music teachers to move into positions of senior management. It can be all too easy for schools to unintentionally marginalize subjects that are not at the heart of the curriculum.

Today one might more commonly find this kind of department:

The music department is integrated well with most areas of the school. Although the department is in a separate block music permeates the life of the school, through performances in assemblies, impromptu performances of extra-curricular groups for other students and a series of community workshops. The music department has a very high reputation with parents and the local community. There are several music teachers. Some are full-time class specialists, others are visiting tutors. All staff contribute to extra-curricular activities. The department has devised a successful assessment policy and this is now being trailed in other departments. The department has strong links with schools in Sweden, France and the USA. There have been recent projects with a local university and a joint performance of a newly commissioned piece of music theatre. There is also good liaison with a local special school and GCSE and A level students have the opportunity to work either with a music therapist, or in a nursery school. One teacher teaches Year 6 students at a local primary school. Another teacher runs a Samba workshop for parents. Each year the department has a composer in residence for one week and has benefited from workshops with orchestras, jazz musicians and a Bhangra band. The head of department is a recent appointment, since the previous post holder was promoted. The links with higher education, opportunities for experiencing music therapy and regular use of visiting composers have all been planned and developed over a period of time. The department has further development plans.

Music's place within the curriculum

The inclusion of music within the National Curriculum has provided us with a good opportunity to make a case for why music should be taught and why it can make a very strong contribution to many areas of school life. There has occasionally been a tendency for music educators to present music as something that is special, mysterious and which requires a special talent. This approach is less common today. While it is true that music is special and important, it will not help our case if we present it as being only accessible to a few. We need to be clear about what music has to offer and make sure that we make others, such as parents, employers and teaching staff, aware of it.

The music National Curriculum Orders are very helpful:

The importance of music
Music is a powerful, unique form of communication that can change the way students feel, think and act. It brings together intellect and feeling and enables personal expression, reflection and emotional development. As an integral part of culture, past and present, it helps students to understand themselves and to relate to others, forging important links between the home, school and the wider world. The teaching of music develops students' ability

> *to listen and appreciate a wide variety of music and to make judgements about musical quality. It encourages active involvement in different forms of amateur music making, both individual and communal, developing a sense of group identity and togetherness. It also increases self-discipline and creativity, aesthetic sensitivity and fulfilment.*
>
> (1999: 14)

This statement provides an ideal starting point for departmental aims and objectives. A careful balance will need to be maintained between the particular contribution music can make to a student's education, and what music education can do to enhance other subjects, key skills or aspects of a student's educational experience. The prime reason for music's place within a school curriculum is its unique character. There is a constant need to market music as a useful commodity in the life of schools and the wider community. Every piece of research confirming music's contribution to key skills, aesthetic development, or anything else, is a useful propaganda tool. If music educators do not seize the opportunity to make use of this information no one else will.

Key skills

Key skills are required in all areas of the curriculum, the world of work and for life beyond education. They enable students to access information, utilize it and apply it to new contexts. This is an important requirement and considered by many to be essential for employment in the modern world. The National Curriculum Orders once again provide helpful information about some of the ways this might be achieved:

> **Promoting key skills through music**
> *For example, music provides opportunities for students to develop the key skills of:*
>
> - **Communication**, *through presenting music to different audiences, and discussing and sharing ideas with others*
> - **Application of number**, *through recognizing pattern, sequence, order and rhythmic relationships*
> - **Information technology**, *through using a range of ICT to compose and perform music*
> - **Working with others**, *through taking different roles and recognizing and supporting the different contributions of others in group and ensemble work*
> - **Improving own learning and performance**, *through appraising their own work, recognizing the need for perseverance, developing the ability to use time effectively, and increasing their ability to work independently*
> - **Problem solving**, *through achieving intentions when composing and presenting performances to different audiences and in different venues.*
>
> (1999: 8)

It may be helpful to include information about these skills within a departmental handbook or policy document. Short and medium-term planning might benefit from having these areas included so that opportunities are mapped and developed whenever possible.

Literacy in Key Stage 3
Music can make a strong contribution to the use of language by ensuring that students:

■ express themselves correctly and appropriately
■ read accurately and with understanding
■ use correct spelling and punctuation
■ follow grammatical conventions
■ organize their writing in logical and coherent forms
■ speak precisely and cogently
■ listen to others and respond to their ideas
■ learn strategies that help them to read with understanding
■ follow a process or argument
■ synthesize and adapt what they have read
■ use specialist vocabulary.

Music lessons will predominantly consist of the manipulation or appraisal of sounds. It can therefore be tempting to dismiss, or give insufficient consideration, to the contribution that music can offer to these other areas of the curriculum. One of the reasons for this may be that we want to celebrate the special nature of music and think of it as being different to other subjects. This is understandable. But music can also offer rich opportunities for developing areas such as literacy. These areas are considered important, and if we ignore them we may unintentionally help to marginalize music's place in schools. We will need to maintain a careful balance in the curriculum between the development of musical skills and using reasonable opportunities to contribute to other areas. It is important that other staff, including senior managers, are aware of the contributions that music is making to key skills such as literacy.

Literacy skills can be developed at Key Stage 3 by:

■ including in schemes of work a list of key vocabulary for each project
■ putting up, and referring to, classroom displays which make use of 'key vocabulary'
■ encouraging students to make use of technical terms when describing their performances, compositions or music they listen to
■ giving students opportunities to evaluate each others' work. For example *when listening to each others' compositions or performances asking students to indicate areas for improvement using carefully considered language.*

There can be tensions between whole-school developments, such as literacy, and the desire for particular musical aims. For example *a teacher works with a Year 7 class on instruments of the orchestra. The students spend six weeks on this project and they do not perform or compose any music during this time. The school believes that this project is a good example of the contribution that music makes to literacy skills. However, the range of strategies used for developing literacy skills is quite limited and most of the activity does not make a strong contribution to musical skills. This project needs to be reviewed in order to achieve a better balance between writing and active engagement with music.*

A successful approach will often ensure that although the key focus of an activity is musical opportunities will be taken to maximize the impact that music can make to other key areas, without compromising the musicality of the task. It is helpful if these activities are planned but opportunities may also be taken as they arise.

Developing literacy with examination classes

Examination classes provide many good opportunities for developing literacy skills. Post-16 students, for example, are capable of using language in a very effective way and of developing their critical skills by considering how other writers use language. In chapter 9, information was given about ways to integrate activities. Beethoven's 1st Symphony (introduction) was taken as an example. This could be extended still further. For example:

A level students are encouraged to carry out an analysis of the use of language in classic music texts. They are asked to consider the use of language in Tovey's writing on the Beethoven 1st Symphony. They start by choosing key words and using a thesaurus to suggest synonyms:

Words used by Tovey	Associated words in a thesaurus
Mysterious	*Invisible, uncertain, obscure, concealed*
Triumph	*Rejoicing, great success, victory, celebration*

They use this as a basis to ask some questions about the use of language when describing music:

1. *How precise is Tovey in describing the listener's experience?*
2. *What does he mean by the word 'triumph'?*
3. *Statements about music need to be supported by evidence. How effective is Tovey at doing this?*
4. *In one sentence summarize Tovey's views on this piece.*
5. *Tovey describes this piece as having a 'grand note of triumph'. How should he argue this case logically and how can this be supported by musical exemplification?*

From this exercise students become aware of how:

■ *difficult it is to be precise with language*
■ *words can imply multiple meanings and value judgements*
■ *important it is to ensure that descriptive statements about music are supported by clear evidence.*

The students go on to consider the ' identity' of a piece of music, considered from the differing points of view provided by the:

■ *composer's intentions*
■ *musical structure*
■ *listener's response*
■ *performer.*

They look at different writers' approaches to musical description and criticism:

> *Only after much experimentation and many sketches did Beethoven venture before the public with his first symphony ... originality is found here, within the conventional symphonic idiom. To begin the work with a seventh chord was an original touch; to write a slow introduction for the last movement was also unusual.*
>
> Pauly 1973: 191

> *Theories about art are useless unless they are based on observation of actual works of art, and any theory of the symphony must begin with the truism that the greatest symphonies were composed by Beethoven. The sonata idea depends on the discovery that large structures may be erected on the basis of tonal relations, as may be seen by examining the earliest examples where themes are mere formulas and polyphony is banished, not through lack of skill, but because the harmonic tensions generated are incompatible with the setting of designs based on simple triadic relations.*
>
> Lam 1966: 104

They use these texts to analyse the stance that the writer has taken when writing about a piece of music:

Some critical approaches	Evidence of this approach
Musical sounds	
Social context	
Formal structure	
Feelings or senses of the listener	

This analysis of the use of language helps the students to develop a more effective approach to the use of language in their own description and essay writing. They are also asked to re-write a passage in order to give it greater clarity:

> *Beethoven's powers of composition are almost entirely concerned here with this extending of the stress-bearing capacity of the harmonic architecture. Once grasp this, with its consequent prospects of changing the whole classical style from the perfected comedy of manners (which is not superficial whether in Haydn or Mozart, or in Pope's couplets) to what is sometimes vaguely, if impressively described as cosmic drama, and we shall not commit the folly of carping at Beethoven's plainness of materials in other respects.*
>
> Lam 1966: 111

This task encourages the students to test their understanding of the set work and to consider how, when writing about music, clarity of expression is very important. They re-write extracts from each others' essays in order to practise this further.

The school ethos

Most subject areas have the potential to make a contribution to the ethos of a school. This can occur through:

- opportunities taken within the curriculum
- out-of-class activities
- the relationship between teachers and students
- the relationship between teachers and other teachers
- the example set by teachers or older students.

Music can play a very strong role in the development of this important area of school life. It may be helpful to include information on how this will be done in the departmental handbook, policy or scheme of work.

Spiritual development

Spiritual development is likely to occur when students are encouraged to go beyond the mechanics of a piece of music and start to reflect on:

- the beauty and wonder of music
- how they are moved by music
- how music can be used to express spiritual ideas (particularly when associated with religious or spiritual texts).

This can occur with any age group. For example:

- *a Year 8 class considers the plight of victims of the atomic bomb at Hiroshima when working on a composition project based on the work of Penderecki. They discuss their own emotional response to this event and consider some of the ways in which the music expresses these*
- *a group of Year 11 students considers some of the ways that different composers have set the religious words Agnus Dei qui tollis peccata mundi. They consider works by Bach, Britten, Byrd, Stravinsky and Haydn*
- *Year 13 students consider the conflict between the artistic aims of Mozart, his personality and the society in which he worked. They look at 'The Marriage of Figaro' and study the social context of servant and master relationships, the political climate of the day and the personal circumstances of Mozart.*

Moral development

Moral development can occur with any year group. Students are likely to consider:

- some of the ways music can cause a nuisance in particular circumstances, for example *through high noise levels*
- moral issues raised in some music. For example *through words of songs, settings of particular texts, the use of language in popular music*
- the celebration of music from different settings, styles, places and cultures, for example *the value judgements placed on music from different cultures*
- common value judgements made about different styles of music and musicians, for example *the images promoted of pop musicians and orchestral musicians*
- the changing roles of men and women within society and how this is reflected in the roles they have played in music making. For example *the relative lack of women composers in the development of classical music.*

Social development

Social development can be approached in two ways:

1. The development of students' social skills through participation in group work, discussion and effective co-operation.
2. The consideration of how music reflects different aspects of society.

Students may:

- consider how music can add to social occasions. For example *music within school assembly, anthems, pop culture, state occasions and ceremony*
- consider how these effects are achieved

■ develop sensitivity to others' views about music. For example *showing an understanding of why someone may appreciate a particular piece of music*

■ consider important social issues such as commercial images, music of ethnic minorities, the under representation of women composers and women performers in particular styles of music and society. For example *Year 12 students research contemporary women composers when studying Brahms. They look at the music of Clara Schumann and evaluate why her music is under-represented in concerts today, how difficult it was for women to have their compositions performed and some of the social reasons for this*

■ consider how music reflects society. As society changes, musical styles and tastes change. For example *punk music as a reaction to the commercialization of popular music.*

Cultural development

Music works within a strong cultural framework. The word 'culture' is often used to mean different things. Clarity over which meaning is being used is often helpful.

1. Improvement through culture

Cultural development is sometimes used to mean some kind of 'improving' quality. A consequence of this stance can be that a particular culture is better than, or higher than another. Cultural development is therefore viewed as an initiation into something with quality. For example *students listen to examples of classical music in order that they will be culturally 'improved' or 'enriched'.* There is often an underlying assumption that other types of music, such as pop music are of a culturally inferior quality. This raises social and moral questions. For example:

■ is it possible to say that one musical style is culturally superior to another?
■ whose judgement about this is correct?
■ does listening to a piece of music, or participating in a performance improve a person?

2. Culture as a context for society

A broader view of culture might attempt to take a more neutral stance in terms of the value judgement placed on a work of art, or artistic activity. A culture will be seen as a reflection, or celebration of a people, and their customs or traditions. Music reflects these cultural contexts. It can also influence them. Cultural traditions are constantly changing and developing over time. This is an outcome of changes in society, cultural contexts and the way humans interact. For example *students consider the changing roles of brass bands in communities where mines have closed or the influence of the Catholic church on choral music of the 17th century.*

3. Multi-cultural awareness

A logical outcome of this broader view is a consideration of music from different countries. Care needs to be taken about how this is presented. For example *it is all too easy to give the impression that Indian music can be covered in four weeks. Indian music is a hugely complex area and includes many different styles. It can no more be covered in four weeks than Western classical music.* This kind of approach has the potential to place a value judgement on particular styles or cultures. 'Unimportant' cultures are covered superficially and not given appropriate status. It is often most helpful to have an approach which demonstrates how different countries and traditions have common links, rather than an implication of difference, which can be implied by a superficial look at 'other' cultures.

Promoting cultural development through music

Effective cultural development in music might therefore have these features:

- students reflect on how music from other cultures can use similar musical devices, yet achieve different effects and cultural identity
- they experience and begin to value music from a variety of styles
- they begin to value music from a variety of cultures.

It may be helpful to see these areas as something to be integrated into all aspects of a departmental scheme of work. This will mean that planning does not include sections on African music, or Indian music. Instead the teacher takes every opportunity to include examples from different cultures and traditions into all projects. For example *Year 7 students have worked on compositions based on different pentatonic scales. As part of this project they have listened to examples of music from the western classical tradition, India, Africa, folk traditions and from pop.*

This approach can be taken throughout Years 7–13. In this way students encounter a range of different musical styles and cultures, presented in a context which celebrates their common links.

Vocational relevance

Music is a multi-million pound business. Most students will listen to music and spend a considerable proportion of their financial resources buying recordings or attending live concerts. Despite this, music in schools can sometimes appear to be an irrelevance to some of these students. Much can be done to make them aware of the benefits of music in society. In particular it may be helpful to give them information about:

- careers in the music industry
- careers in associated industries
- the contribution music makes to society (entertainment, employment, therapy, economics and so on)
- the role music plays in films, television and advertising
- the images put forward by different musicians (classical, popular, easy-listening, folk and so on).

Although a particularly useful time to do this would be at moments in a student's life when they are considering career options and examination course choices, it may be helpful to ensure that the relevance of music to society and the world of employment is promoted wherever possible. There are many careers where the skills developed during music lessons can be very important. Some students may have come to the conclusion that music is only relevant for the talented few. If this is the case, music will run the risk of always being a minority examination subject.

Essential skills for the modern musician

Students who increasingly specialize in music, for example *taking music examination courses or instrumental exams,* can be encouraged to become aware of the need to develop a range of associated skills required by modern musicians. For example:

- diary organization and management
- marketing and promotion
- production of publicity materials
- effective practise techniques
- concert management
- writing programme notes
- presenting concerts so that they are accessible to a wide range of listeners
- budgeting and fund-raising
- concert and tour organization
- risk assessment.

Many of these tasks will require mediation by a teacher, or some other adult. However these are the kind of skills which students will find useful if they move into higher education or employment, whether in music or not. There are many rich opportunities for students' development, which can be taken both within schools and in other settings, for example *the youth orchestra.*

Summary points:
Music can make a strong contribution to many aspects of a student's development. In order to maximize these opportunities, it will be helpful if they are mapped and planned as part of medium and short-term planning. They may also be included as part of a departmental handbook or policy document (if appropriate). Opportunities can be taken with all year groups and in many out-of-class opportunities.

Self-review and improvement

Aim: this chapter provides a framework for self-review. It is intended that this can be used on a regular basis in order to set targets for further improvement.

▨ The need for self-review

The teacher who is able to review their work honestly and critically is likely to improve. Effective self-evaluation is most likely to occur when it is done regularly and is followed by identified targets for improvement, appropriate professional development and an in-built further review of progress.

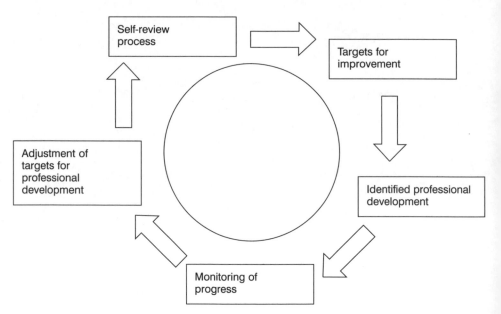

The Handbook for Inspecting Secondary Schools (1999: 138) suggests four questions and three points for action that are at the heart of self-evaluation:

1. Are all students in my school learning as much as they are capable of learning?
2. What can I do to find out?
3. When I answer this question how do I know I am right?
4. What do I do about it when I have the answer?

To ensure that self-evaluation has the maximum impact on standards:

■ take an objective look at students' achievements and pinpoint areas of underachievement

■ account for outcomes in your school by identifying strengths and weaknesses in teaching, before looking at what else you provide to support learning

■ use this information to devise the School Improvement (Development Plan), which is at its best when seen simply as a means to raise standards.

Although written in the context of reviewing the work of the whole-school, these points provide us with a useful starting point for departmental self-review.

The benefits of a review process

Teaching is a busy and stressful occupation. It can, thankfully, also be exhilarating, exciting and rewarding. One factor which can make it more stressful is when insufficient attention is given to professional development needs and the priorities required for future improvement. It is sometimes difficult to step back and take an objective look at what we are doing, because the pace of change never seems to slow, new initiatives come along on a regular basis and life seems too hectic. If you feel like this you may believe that you have not got time to review your work. If so, you may run the risk of not improving. As a rule, teachers set themselves high aspirations and want to improve their work.

As part of the Performance Management initiative teachers will need to provide evidence that they:

■ *take responsibility for their professional development and use the outcomes to improve their teaching and students' learning.*

(1999: 5)

It is helpful to have the opportunity to discuss your work and professional development with someone else, using them as a catalyst for change and development. This can be:

- informative
- illuminating
- interesting
- inspiring
- challenging.

The process should help you to:

- prioritize what you are doing
- cut out inessential activity
- be more coherent about planning
- gain greater control over your work.

It could also save you time in the long term.

Identifying needs

There are four main ways of doing this:

1. Review with senior managers.
2. Review using advisory services or other consultants.
3. Inspection.
4. Self-review.

All these methods are useful, and an ideal scenario would involve all of them within a planned cycle.

Courses

Courses are very useful. They enable you to step back from your work and consider some broader points and how they might impact on your work. They give you the chance to meet other people and talk about aspects of your work. They provide the opportunity to pool ideas and feel reassurance that others share any worries you have. They can sometimes be really inspiring. Courses are, necessarily, often quite general and may not touch on the specific concerns you have. To be successful they will need you to:

- be clear that the course is targeted at your need. For example *it is unrealistic to expect a course-leader to address your specific concerns if the course has clearly not aimed to do this in the first place*
- take away any points or information and be prepared to apply them to your own, unique situation. A course can not provide easy answers which meet everyone's needs.

Inspection as a form of review

All schools are inspected at least every six years using a framework laid down by OFSTED (The Office for Standards in Education). The framework is an open document, which is publicly available and aspires to involve schools in a process of improvement through inspection. It can be a useful tool for self-review. What you gain from the experience of an inspection or review will very much depend on your approach to it. The inspection process involves judgements. This is so that the information fed back to schools and parents is unambiguous. It is possible to learn a lot from the experience by listening carefully to what is being said, even if you think you do not agree with it. A good inspector will give clear feedback about strengths and weaknesses. This is useful information. Listen and accept that we all have areas where we need to improve and develop. It may be helpful to try to think of the process as being a partnership that has the same aim, rather than being an intrusion from outside. The inspector is trying to improve the quality of the students' educational experience. This is the same aim as the teacher.

Music teachers quite often work in single person departments. When the department is inspected, it may feel like the inspector is there for a lot of the time. There are, however, some advantages to this:

- a teacher's work is known well by the inspector
- there is an opportunity for informal as well as formal contact
- there is an opportunity to build up some form of working relationship with the inspector.

Inspection is probably best viewed as a health check to confirm how things are going. It complements the department's self-review process, and offers a useful outside audit of what is happening.

Documentation required for inspection and self-review

The following is a list of information or documentation that will be useful for any sort of review process. This includes inspections.

1. Departmental timetable (even if the department consists of one person). Include where possible the timetables of all visiting instrumental/vocal teachers.
2. Schemes of work. Schools will obviously vary in the amount of detail included. Some give a very brief outline, while others give a detailed breakdown of each lesson. The quality is definitely more important than the quantity. The documentation should include your aims and objectives, as well as a broad idea of how your schemes will address the Key Stage 3 Programmes of Study. Remember that a scheme should be available for Key Stage 4 and post-16. An examination syllabus is not a scheme of work. See chapter 2 for more information on schemes of work.

3. Many schools have useful policy documents which incorporate their schemes of work. They might also state the school's policy on the teaching of music (agreed by the governors).
4. Copies of reports. It is helpful to consider copies of reports for students who receive instrumental lessons.
5. Tape recordings of compositions in each Key Stage, if available. **There is no expectation that these will be available or that you should be making tape recordings.** However, this evidence is very helpful because it provides an insight into work that has taken place prior to the review or inspection, and gives a more secure feel for what happens in the school over the rest of the year.
6. Departmental policy on the teaching of students with special needs, including the more able. Does the department keep copies of individual learning plans? It is helpful to point out to an inspector any students in a lesson whom you consider to be particularly able, or those who are on the special needs register.
7. Information about the financial allocation given to music, how the money is spent and how priorities are planned. How is the sum of money arrived at? For example *formula, bids, combination*.
8. Information about recent professional development and how the priorities for development are planned. It is often helpful to include this within a departmental development plan so that clear links can be seen.
9. Information about any recent special events such as concerts, workshops and so on. The inspection or review should focus mostly on the teaching and learning of all students and not just the minority who might take part in extra-curricular activities. Have any of these groups been monitored to note any gender imbalances? What steps, if any, have been taken to address these?
10. A list of departmental resources and plans for future developments, if available.
11. Information about the ways that students are assessed and records of these assessments. For example:

   ■ extracts from the teacher's mark book
   ■ the school's End of Key Stage 3 Assessments and how they compare to national or local data
   ■ examination results and a comparison with national/local results
   ■ information on how well these students did in other subjects
   ■ information about the criteria that are used to award grades and how these criteria relate to any whole school policy
   ■ information about how instrumental lessons are assessed.

   (For more information on assessment see chapter 3).

12. The governors' policy on the provision of instrumental or vocal tuition. Who has access to this tuition and is there a charging policy? Have the governors monitored the uptake by gender and ethnicity? Has an assessment been made of the contribution this makes to attainment, set in the context of the cost and other resources allocated to music?
13. For examination groups, it is helpful to provide any information from examination boards on course marks and break-down by papers. Are students scoring consistently better or worse in one particular element of the examination? See chapter 8 for more information.
14. The previous inspection report and any information on support and development that has taken place since then. This will probably include information on how any issues for development in the previous report have been addressed.

Self-review

The following self-review questionnaire is designed to be used as a diagnostic tool for identification of development priorities and training needs. It can be used individually or, ideally, with a colleague. It is quite comprehensive. It might be best to take one section and work on that first of all. A lot of detail has been included so that the evaluation can be thorough, and there will be value in you returning to it at a later date. You do not need to complete it all in one attempt. The information will be useful if you are involved in a performance management review.

Stage 1

Decide on the areas that you want to cover and look at the questions and evaluation criteria. In the evidence box write down some specific examples of where you think that area has been covered. For example:

Attainment Key Stage 3	Evidence
What evidence is there that students play instruments with control of dynamics and pulse?	*They can alter how they play an instrument in order to create the effect they want. For example, in the project on dynamics Year 8 created a piece with a loud section and a quiet section. They controlled the pulse of this piece and understood the importance of dynamic contrast.*

You may decide that your students could do more to evaluate the quality of the sound they make and the use of more subtle dynamics. You therefore write this information in the evidence box and score 2 (fair). You think this is quite good but are aware that it could be improved further.

It is important that you fill in the information on the questionnaire honestly. Do not be too hard on yourself, but be honest if there are areas you feel could be improved. Some examples have been provided for clarification. Now make a list of areas you feel could be improved and give them an order of priority. Some will have a 2, or even a 3. These may suggest themselves as a priority.

Stage 2

Choose two or three things that you could work on during the next year. Be realistic, choose things which you know you can improve and set yourself a clear target which you can measure at the end of a specified time. In doing this you will need to consider:

- the resources needed
- professional development (course or working with someone coming into school)
- who needs to know about the target (other members of the department, governors, senior management, students, parents)
- how this will link to appraisal
- how it will be integrated into your departmental development plan.

Stage 3

It might be helpful to put these onto a planning sheet. This can be used for monitoring (for example *plotting your progress in six months' time*) and as a starting point for the following year's self-review process. It may be helpful to share these plans with an inspector if your department is inspected. A typical plan might look like this:

Date	Success criteria (what will have happened when this has been completed). When will this be done?	Who is responsible?	Professional development needs	Other resources needed
Target 1				
Target 2				
Target 3				

You now have a useful agenda for your own professional development for the near future. Discuss this with your senior manager, and decide how to address these areas.

The following pages provides a useful checklist for self-review.

Educational outcomes

Evaluation criteria ATTAINMENT Key Stage 3	Evidence			Score
What evidence is there that students:	Possible sources of evidence that the students can do this: ● asking students to describe what they know and understand (in ways which are appropriate for their age) ● audio or video recordings ● written evidence (such as scores or descriptions of their work) ● lesson observations ● asking students to listen to music (either their own or commercial recordings) and describing what they can hear			1 = strong 2 = fair 3 = weak
● sing expressively a variety of songs (including two parts) with expression and feeling?				
● play instruments expressively? For example *they can l isten to others whilst performing their own part, adjust their part and show sensitivity in performance*				
● sing with control of pitch? For example *the large majority sing in tune when performing a variety of different pieces including songs with two or more parts*				

Evaluation criteria ATTAINMENT Key Stage 3	Evidence	Score
• play instruments with control of dynamics and pulse? For example *they can alter how they play an instrument in order to create the effect they want; they listen to the sound they make and make adjustments in order to obtain the effect they want*		
• compose pieces which show understanding of melody, harmony, accompaniment? For example *they use musical ideas to create the effect they want, for example chord clusters to create a particular effect or choose the sonority of a particular instrument in order to obtain a desired effect*		
• compose pieces which use structure effectively? For example *the structure of the piece has been planned and evaluated against the intended effect, for example students listen to a piece of music and make adjustments to their own composition in order to create a more musical effect*		
• are able to hear and understand music? For example *they can recognize melody and accompaniment in a range of musical styles and cultures, for example they can hear that music can have different textures such as bass, riff, chords, counter melody, polyphony*		

Evaluation criteria ATTAINMENT Key Stage 3	Evidence	Score
• use appropriate technical vocabulary? For example they understand and use terms such as melody, chord, seventh, homophonic and can relate these to music they perform, compose and listen to		
• begin to show an awareness of when pieces were composed and how the context affects the style? For example they can listen to pieces and make approximate judgements about the period in which the pieces were written		
• can analyse and plan to improve their compositions? For example they can talk about the sections of a composition using musical vocabulary such as melody, chord, cluster and understand how these elements affect the quality of their piece		
• by the end of Year 9 most students' attainment is around level 5 of the music National Curriculum Level Descriptions?		
• attainment is at a similar level to the SCAA/QCA exemplification materials?		

Evaluation criteria ATTAINMENT Key Stage 3	Evidence	Score
• are developing their speaking skills through music? *For example they can talk about music using descriptive words and appropriate musical vocabulary*		
• are developing their writing skills through music? *For example they can write down ideas about music they play and hear using musical terms which they understand*		
• are developing their ICT skills through music? *For example they use computer programs to help them store and develop their compositions. They use technology to adjust sounds in order to create the desired effect. They make judgements about when it is and is not appropriate to use technology*		
• are developing their numeracy skills through music?		

Evaluation criteria ATTAINMENT Key Stage 4	Evidence			Score
What evidence is there that students:	Possible sources of evidence that the students can do this: ● asking students to describe what they know and understand (in ways which are appropriate for their age) ● audio or video recordings ● written evidence (such as scores or descriptions of their work) ● lesson observations ● asking students to listen to music (either their own or commercial recordings) and describing what they can hear.			1 = strong 2 = fair 3 = weak
● sing expressively using head and chest voice to create a desired effect?				
● play instruments expressively? For example *they can perform pieces which are rhythmically secure, expressively played and show evidence of musical understanding. They choose pieces that enable them to perform expressively within their own technical capabilities*				
● sing with control of pitch? For example *they can begin to make their own judgements about tuning and how to adjust it. Are aware of the technique required to control pitch*				

Evaluation criteria ATTAINMENT Key Stage 4	Evidence	Score
• play instruments with control, expression and technical competence?		
• compose pieces which show understanding of various tonalities and musical styles?		
• compose pieces which use structure effectively? For example *the structure of the piece makes a substantial contribution to the overall effect*		
• are able to hear and understand music? For example *they can recognize features of music such as the accompaniment, fugue, canon, riff and place these within an historical context*		
• use appropriate technical vocabulary? For example *they can use words which describe music effectively; they talk about raga, development of theme, effect of particular dissonance*		
• they can listen to music and make comments about when it was composed and how the circumstances in which it was composed affects how it sounds?		

Evaluation criteria ATTAINMENT Key Stage 4	Evidence						Score
• can analyse and plan to improve their compositions? For example *they relate their own pieces to music they listen to and begin to understand how music can be made more effective; they decide to transpose a section to give greater tonal variety, experiment with a more varied harmonic style using ninth chords*							
• produce compositions which make full use of their musical understanding?							
• are reaching similar attainment levels to other examination subjects?							
• are developing their speaking skills through music? For example *they can talk about music using descriptive words and appropriate musical vocabulary*							
• are developing their writing skills through music? For example *they can write down ideas about music they play and hear using musical terms which they understand*							
• are developing their ICT skills through music? For example *they use computer programs to help them store and develop their compositions)*							
• are developing their numeracy skills through music?							

Evaluation criteria ATTAINMENT post-16	Evidence	Score
What evidence is there that students:	Possible sources of evidence that the students can do this: • asking students to describe what they know and understand (in ways which are appropriate for their age) • audio or video recordings • written evidence (such as scores or descriptions of their work) • lesson observations • asking students to listen to music (either their own or commercial recordings) and describing what they can hear.	1 = strong 2 = fair 3 = weak
• sing expressively using head and chest voice to create a desired effect?		
• play instruments expressively? For example *they can perform pieces which are rhythmically secure, expressively played and show evidence of musical understanding; they choose pieces which enable them to perform expressively within their own technical capabilities; they adjust performances in order to respond to the context of the composition, for example performing a baroque piece with attention to contemporary performance practice*		

Evaluation criteria ATTAINMENT post-16	Evidence	Score
• sing with control of pitch? For example. *they can make their own judgements about tuning and how to adjust it; they are aware of the technique required to control pitch; they begin to adjust their sound as appropriate, for example, choosing to sing a piece of gospel music with idiomatic tone and diction*		
• play instruments with control, expression and technical competence?		
• compose pieces which show understanding of various tonalities and musical styles? For example *select music from a variety of periods, styles or cultures and show musical understanding of the contexts in which they were composed*		
• compose pieces which use structure effectively – the structure of the piece makes a substantial contribution to the overall effect of the piece For example *they consider alternative structures and make choices based on the piece's effectiveness and intended outcome*		
• are able to hear and understand music? For example *can recognize features of music such as ground bass, dodecaphonic, late romantic, neo-classicism and place these within an historical context*		

Evaluation criteria ATTAINMENT post-16	Evidence	Score
• use appropriate technical vocabulary? For example *talk about raga, neopolitan sixth, alberti bass*		
• can listen to music and make comments about when it was composed and how the circumstances in which it was composed affects how it sounds?		
• analyse and plan to improve their compositions? For example *they relate their own pieces to music they listen to and understand how music can be made more effective; they try alternatives and consider the musical effect*		
• produce compositions which make full use of their musical understanding?		
• are reaching similar attainment levels to other examination subjects?		

Evaluation criteria ATTAINMENT post-16	Evidence	Score
• are developing their speaking skills through music? For example *they can talk about music using descriptive words and appropriate musical vocabulary*		
• are developing their writing skills through music? For example *they can write down ideas about music they play and hear using musical terms which they understand; their essays are clear, closely argued and effective in communicating ideas and understanding; they relate biographical detail to the sound of the music and its expressive qualities; they look critically at the writing of others and consider a range of sources*		
• are developing their IT skills through music? For example *they use a wide range of technology in order to deepen their musical understanding; CD-ROMs are used for research and evaluation, a wide range of technology (including keyboards and sound modules) helps them to evaluate the effect of musical decisions and computer programmes (such as sequencers) enable them to develop and refine their musical ideas*		
• are developing their numeracy skills through music?		

Evaluation criteria LEARNING at Key Stage 3	Evidence	Score
What evidence is there that:	Possible sources of evidence that the students can do this: • work from Year 6 through to Year 9 • tapes or video recordings • lesson observations • notated scores students have made of their compositions	1 = strong 2 = fair 3 = weak
• all students make good progress during lessons?		
• all students make good progress over the period of a year?		
• higher attaining students make good progress?		
• lower attaining students make good progress?		

Evaluation criteria LEARNING at Key Stage 3	Evidence	Score
• students with statements make good progress?		
• girls make good progress?		
• boys make good progress?		
• students who receive instrumental tuition use their skills effectively in class lessons?		
• students in Year 7 are working at a higher level than in Year 6?		
• students in Year 8 are working at a higher level than in Year 7?		

Evaluation criteria LEARNING at Key Stage 3	Evidence	Score
• students in Year 9 are working at a higher level than in Year 8?		
• students from all ethnic groups make good progress?		
• students develop singing skills between Years 7 and 9?		
• students develop performance skills on an instrument (s) between Years 7 and 9?		
• the skills students develop enable all of them to consider GCSE music as a possible option?		

Evaluation criteria LEARNING at Key Stage 4	Evidence	Score
What evidence is there that:	Possible sources of evidence that the students can do this: • work from Year 9 through to Year 11 • teachers records from Years 7–8 • tapes or video recordings • lesson observations • notated scores students have made of their compositions.	1 = strong 2 = fair 3 = weak
• all students make good progress during lessons?		
• all students make good progress over the period of a year?		
• higher attaining students make good progress?		
• lower attaining students make good progress?		
• students with statements make good progress?		

Evaluation criteria LEARNING at Key Stage 4	Evidence	Score
• girls make good progress?		
• boys make good progress?		
• students who receive instrumental tuition use their skills effectively in class lessons? For example *in their instrumental lessons students develop a wide range of skills including improvisation, listening and appraising*		
• students in Year 10 are working at a higher level than in Year 9?		
• students in Year 11 are working at a higher level than in Year 10?		
• students from all ethnic groups make good progress?		

Evaluation criteria LEARNING post-16	Evidence	Score
What evidence is there that:	Possible sources of evidence that the students can do this: • work from Year 2 through to Year 6 • class teachers records from Years 2–6 • tapes or video recordings • lesson observations • notated scores students have made of their compositions.	1 = strong 2 = fair 3 = weak
• all students make good progress during lessons?		
• all students make good progress over the period of a year?		
• higher attaining students make good progress?		
• lower attaining students make good progress?		
• students with statements make good progress?		

Evaluation criteria LEARNING post-16	Evidence	Score
• girls make good progress?		
• boys make good progress?		
• students who receive instrumental tuition use their skills effectively in class lessons? *e.g. in their instrumental lessons students develop a wide range of skills including improvisation, listening and appraising*		
• students in Year 12 are working at a higher level than in Year 11?		
• students in Year 13 are working at a higher level than in Year 12?		
• students from all ethnic groups make good progress?		

Evaluation criteria LEARNING post-16	Evidence	Score
• students can work well independently?		
• students can listen to the work of others?		
• students show respect for instruments and other resources?		
• students can take responsibility? For example *leading a performance*		
• students can maintain co-operative relationships with others?		
• student uptake for GCSE is average or above?		

Evaluation criteria LEARNING post-16	Evidence	Score
• student uptake for A level or other post-16 courses is average or above?		
• students show sensitivity and appreciation to music from a range of styles and cultures?		

Factors contributing to outcomes

Evaluation criteria TEACHING Key Stage 3	Evidence	Score
Factors which contribute to effective teaching:	• your knowledge of your own strengths • information in subject documentation • access to recent staff development • lesson observations.	1 = strong 2 = fair 3 = weak
Subject knowledge Consider: • your knowledge of musical styles and cultures • your awareness of how compositions can create an effect • your use of appropriate questions to ask which will help students to improve their work • your knowledge of how to improve singing skills • your knowledge of how to improve performance skills • ways of starting and developing compositions • ways of linking performing, composing, listening and appraising together • your strengths in subject knowledge • your weaknesses in subject knowledge		
Long-term planning • is there a scheme of work for each year group in the Key Stage? • does the scheme ensure progression between each term and year? • does it go beyond a collection of published resources to be used by the teacher as they see best?		

Evaluation criteria TEACHING Key Stage 3	Evidence	Score
Short-term planning • do lessons have clear learning objectives? • do they relate to the scheme of work? • are they shared with the students? • do they allow for students' different needs? **Methods and strategies** • are all students allowed to feel the success of musical achievement? • are students participating in performances of high musical quality (with attention to musical detail and expression)? • are students participating in compositions of high musical quality (which require them to put into practice their practical skills, knowledge of music and understanding of how it can be expressive)? • are students asked to appraise music of good quality (either their own compositions or commercial recordings) and required to reflect on these performances? • are students required to use their imagination? • are students required to use their initiative? • do students build on the attainment they have developed both in and out of school?		

Evaluation criteria TEACHING Key Stage 3	Evidence	Score
• are students taught to solve technical problems? For example *how to breathe and support singing or how to adjust keyboard sounds in order to create the best effect for a particular purpose* • is notation used only as appropriate and not taught in isolation from other musical activity? • are skills (such as singing) developed regularly and consistently? • is the vocabulary required of students appropriate to the age range and in line with expectations? • do lessons contain a variety of musical activities? **Use of time and resources** • are students encouraged to work to targets in lessons? • are students expected to perform their work regularly? • are activities appropriate for the age range and attention span of students? • are pieces recorded so that compositions completed over several sessions can be stored in order for students to be able to return to ideas with minimum disruption? • do lessons contain activities which have a clear purpose and which collectively add up to a curriculum which ensures continuity, progression and skill development? • are resources deployed and used in the best way? • are the resources used appropriate for the task set? For example *students are not asked to compose pieces which will not work effectively with the resources they have available*		

Evaluation criteria TEACHING Key Stage 4	Evidence	Score
Factors which contribute to effective teaching:	• your knowledge of your own strengths • information in subject documentation • guidance given to class teachers by co-ordinators • access to recent staff development.	1 = strong 2 = fair 3 = weak
Subject knowledge Consider: • your knowledge of musical styles and cultures • your awareness of how compositions can create an effect • your use of appropriate questions to ask which will help students to improve their work • your knowledge of how to improve singing skills • your knowledge of how to improve performance skills • ways of starting and developing compositions • ways of linking performing, composing, listening and appraising together • your strengths in subject knowledge • your weaknesses in subject knowledge.		
Long-term planning • is there a scheme of work for each year group in the Key Stage? • does the scheme ensure progression between each term and year? • does it go beyond a collection of published resources to be used by the class teacher as they see best?		

Evaluation criteria TEACHING Key Stage 4	Evidence	Score
Short-term planning • do lessons have clear learning objectives? • do they relate to the scheme of work? • are they shared with the students? • do they allow for differentiation? **Methods and strategies** • are all students allowed to feel the success of musical achievement? • are students participating in performances of high musical quality (with attention to pulse, dynamics and timbre)? • are students participating in compositions of high musical quality (which require them to put into practice their practical skills, knowledge of music and understanding of how it can be expressive)? • are students asked to appraise music of good quality (either their own compositions or commercial recordings) and required to reflect on these performances? • are students required to use their imagination? • are students required to use their initiative? • do students build on the attainment they have developed both in and out of school? • are students taught to solve technical problems? For example *how to breathe and support singing or how to cross the thumb when playing keyboards*		

Evaluation criteria TEACHING Key Stage 4	Evidence	Score
• is notation used only as appropriate and not taught in isolation from other musical activity? • are skills (such as singing) developed regularly and consistently? • is the vocabulary required of students appropriate to the age range and in line with expectations? • do lessons contain a variety of musical activities?		
Use of time and resources • are students encouraged to work to targets in lessons? • are students expected to perform their work regularly? • are activities appropriate for the age range and attention span of students? • are pieces recorded so that compositions completed over several sessions can be stored in order for students to be able to return to ideas with minimum disruption? • do lessons contain activities which have a clear purpose and which collectively add up to a curriculum which ensures continuity, progression and skill development? • are resources deployed and used in the best way? For example *students are not asked to only compose pieces with instruments which have a limited timbre*		

Evaluation criteria TEACHING post-16	Evidence	Score
Factors which contribute to effective teaching:	• your knowledge of your own strengths • information in subject documentation • guidance given to class teachers by co-ordinators • access to recent staff development.	1 = strong 2 = fair 3 = weak
Subject knowledge Consider: • your knowledge of musical styles and cultures • your awareness of how compositions can create an effect • your use of appropriate questions to ask which will help students to improve their work • your knowledge of how to improve singing skills • your knowledge of how to improve performance skills • ways of starting and developing compositions • ways of linking performing, composing, listening and appraising together • your strengths in subject knowledge • your weaknesses in subject knowledge.		
Long-term planning • is there a scheme of work for each year group in the Key Stage? • does the scheme ensure progression between each term and year? • is it more than the examination specification?		

Evaluation criteria TEACHING post-16	Evidence	Score
Short-term planning • do lessons have clear learning objectives? • do they relate to the scheme of work? • are they shared with the students? • do they respond to students' differing needs? **Methods and strategies** • are all students allowed to feel the success of musical achievement? • are students participating in performances of high musical quality? • are students participating in compositions of high musical quality? For example *require them to put into practice their practical skills, knowledge of music and understanding of how it can be expressive* • are students asked to appraise music of good quality (either their own compositions or commercial recordings) and required to reflect on these performances? • are students required to use their imagination? • are students required to use their initiative? • do students build on the attainment they have developed both in and out of school? • are students taught to solve technical problems? • are skills (such as singing) developed regularly and consistently?		

Evaluation criteria TEACHING post-16	Evidence	Score
• is the vocabulary required of students appropriate to the age range and in line with expectations? • do lessons contain a variety of musical activities? • are activities integrated well?		
Use of time and resources • are students encouraged to work to targets in lessons? • are students expected to perform their work regularly? • are activities appropriate for the age range and attention span of students? • are pieces recorded so that compositions completed over several sessions can be stored in order for students to be able to return to ideas with minimum disruption? • do lessons contain activities which have a clear purpose and which collectively add up to a curriculum which ensures continuity, progression and skill development? • are resources deployed and used in the best way? • are the resources used appropriate for the task set?		

Evaluation criteria CURRICULUM AND ASSESSMENT Key Stage 3	Evidence	Score
Quality of curriculum organization and arrangements for assessment:	• schemes of work • lesson plans • assessment arrangements • teacher's records.	1 = strong 2 = fair 3 = weak
• is the amount of curriculum time available sufficient to fulfil the requirements of the National Curriculum (guidelines are 45 hours each year)?		
• is it organized so that students can make and sustain progress in: – singing skills? – playing instruments? – composing pieces which make use of their musical knowledge and understanding? – listening to music from a variety of styles and cultures in order to note particular features? – appraising music from a variety of styles and cultures in order to make judgements about important musical features?		
• are activities such as whole-school hymn singing in addition to the amount of time devoted to music education in the school?		

Evaluation criteria CURRICULUM AND ASSESSMENT Key Stage 3	Evidence	Score
• is there a coherent scheme of work for each year group?		
• is time organized so that students receive regular music sessions and are able to develop and consolidate their musical skills?		
• are regular assessments made of students' work?		
• do the students understand the assessment system and how it is used?		
• is assessment used to inform curriculum planning?		

Evaluation criteria CURRICULUM AND ASSESSMENT Key Stage 3	Evidence	Score
• do lessons encourage integration between performing, composing, listening and appraising?		
• is account taken of work undertaken in each subsequent year?		
• are records kept of students' progress?		
• does the school offer appropriate extra-curricular activities?		
• does the school offer extra tuition on instruments?		

Evaluation criteria CURRICULUM AND ASSESSMENT Key Stage 3	Evidence	Score
• does the school have a clear policy on who has access to instrumental tuition?		
• has any policy on instrumental tuition been approved by the governors?		
• does the school monitor the gender of students who have instrumental lessons?		
• does the school monitor the ethnicity of students who have instrumental lessons?		
• does the school monitor the impact instrumental tuition has on students' attainment?		

Evaluation criteria CURRICULUM AND ASSESSMENT Key Stage 3	Evidence	Score
• do instrumental lessons integrate with and complement class music lessons?		
• does the school offer lessons on instruments from a wide range of styles and cultures?		

Evaluation criteria CURRICULUM AND ASSESSMENT Key Stage 4	Evidence	Score
Quality of curriculum organization and arrangements for assessment:	• schemes of work • lesson plans • assessment arrangements • teacher's records.	1 = strong 2 = fair 3 = weak
• is the amount of curriculum time available sufficient to fulfil the course requirements?		

• is it organised so that students can make and sustain progress in:
  – singing skills?
  – playing instruments?
  – composing pieces which make use of their musical knowledge and understanding?
  – listening to music from a variety of styles and cultures in order to note particular features?
  – appraising music from a variety of styles and cultures in order to make judgements about important musical features?		

• is there a coherent scheme of work for each year group?		

Evaluation criteria CURRICULUM AND ASSESSMENT Key Stage 4	Evidence	Score
• is time organized so that students receive regular music sessions and are able to develop and consolidate their musical skills?		
• are regular assessments made of students' work?		
• do the students understand the assessment system and how it is used?		
• is assessment used to inform curriculum planning?		
• do lessons encourage integration between performing, composing, listening and appraising?		

Evaluation criteria CURRICULUM AND ASSESSMENT Key Stage 4	Evidence	Score
• is account taken of work undertaken in each subsequent year?		
• are records kept of students' progress?		

Evaluation criteria CURRICULUM AND ASSESSMENT post-16	Evidence			Score
Quality of curriculum organisation and arrangements for assessment:	● schemes of work ● lesson plans ● assessment arrangements ● teacher's records.			1 = strong 2 = fair 3 = weak
● is the amount of curriculum time available sufficient to fulfil the course requirements?				
● is it organized so that students can make and sustain progress in: – singing skills? – playing instruments? – composing pieces which make use of their musical knowledge and understanding? – listening to music from a variety of styles and cultures in order to note particular features? – appraising music from a variety of styles and cultures in order to make judgements about important musical features?				
● is there a coherent scheme of work for each year group?				

Evaluation criteria CURRICULUM AND ASSESSMENT post-16	Evidence	Score
• is time organized so that students receive regular music sessions and are able to develop and consolidate their musical skills?		
• are regular assessments made of students' work?		
• do the students understand the assessment system and how it is used?		
• is assessment used to inform curriculum planning?		
• do lessons encourage integration between performing, composing, listening and appraising?		
• are records kept of students' progress?		

Summary points:
It is helpful to review work on a regular basis. This enables the teacher to maintain an agenda for improvement and to ensure that appropriate professional development is identified.

References

BECTA (1998), *Music Technology in Action, The Training Guide*

Brown, H. (1976), *Music in the Renaissance*, Prentice Hall

Bruner, J. S. (1966), *Toward a Theory of Instruction*, Harvard University Press

Department of Education and Science (1985), *Music 5—16, Curriculum Matters 4*, HMSO

DFEE (2000), *Performance Management in Schools*

HMI (1980), *A View of the Curriculum*, HMSO

Lam, B. (1966), *The Symphony: Haydn to Dvorak*, Pelican

OFSTED (1999), *Handbook for Inspecting Secondary Schools*, HMSO

Pauly, R. (1973), *Music in the Classic Period*, Prentice Hall

Paynter, J. (1982), *Music in the Secondary School Curriculum*, Cambridge University Press

QCA (1999), *Music: The National Curriculum for England*

Manhattanville Music Curriculum Program (1970) Bardonia, New York: Media Materials Inc.

Salaman, W. (1983), *Living School Music*, Cambridge University Press

Spencer, P. (1993) 'GCSE Music: A Survey of Undergraduate Opinion', *British Journal of Music Education 10*, pp.73–84

Swanwick, K. (1979), *A Basis for Music Education*, NFER-Nelson, Windsor

Tovey, D. (1972), *Essays in Musical Analysis*, Oxford University Press

Index